WHO I AM
DEPENDS ON ME!

Dunni

WHO I AM
DEPENDS ON ME!

By

Patty Hendrickson

ISBN: 0-9639095-1-7

PATTY HENDRICKSON, Certified Speaking Professional, works with organizations that want to grow leaders and with people who want more out of life. As a keynote speaker and leadership facilitator since 1987, Patty has shared enthusiastic messages throughout the world to more than 100,000 people.

She is the product of intense student activities serving as a National President of a Career and Technical Student Organization (CTSO) and International Officer of a Greek organization. Patty has a Masters of Business Administration and is Past President of the National Speakers Association - Wisconsin Chapter. She has earned the highest designation from the National Speakers Association of Certified Speaking Professional (CSP) – earned by less than 500 people in the world.

If you're looking for an energizing keynote speaker or workshop leader, ask for Patty's free promotional information. *Her energy inspires, so her message sticks!*

Patty Hendrickson
Hendrickson Leadership Group, Inc.
N601 Lost Ridge Rd.
Lacrosse, WI 54601
800-557-2889
Patty@pattyhendrickson.com
www.pattyhendrickson.com

CONTENTS

Value. . .America

Reading. . .Wondering. . .Writing

Inspiring Thoughts 191

ACKNOWLEDGEMENT

An interesting situation occurred while preparing this book for publication . . .

Many quotes and points to ponder have been included for you to enjoy, but these quotes were questioned by those who read the manuscript. People asked me if I was sexist for including quotes that specifically say *man*, *he*, and *his*. (Hmmm?) At one point all of the quotes were changed to show no gender preference, but I had a very difficult time deciding if this was fair to the quoted individual. The quotes are now in their true form — the way they were originally stated.

I apologize if you are offended by this decision. In no way do I condone or believe that these quotes exclude women. The quotes are merely a reflection of words stated in a different time when people were not as conscientious about their use of pronouns in our language and the importance of including all people (both men and women) in their statements. In fact, I think there is a wonderful lesson in the metamorphosis of quotes of many years ago to today. It shows us that enormous changes can occur when all of us do our part, however small that may be, to increase awareness.

I hope you enjoy the quotes and the magical messages they proclaim to every HUMAN BEING!

WHO I AM
DEPENDS ON ME!

Don't forget that everybody, including yourself, has only his own experience to think with.

—Rudolf Flesch

Who I Am Depends on Me!

I am a human being.
I will fail, but I am not a failure.

There is good and bad in this world.
I will do bad things, but I am not bad.

There are right and wrong answers.
I will give wrong answers, but I am not wrong.

I am a collection of ideas, impressions and experiences.
I act upon this collection.
Every creature is a different collection.
We act differently. It's okay.

My failure may be your success.
My bad deed may be your good deed.
My wrong answer may be your right answer.
It's okay, we're different.

I am only responsible for one human being—me.
I know only one collection—my own.
Who I am depends on me!

Patty Hendrickson

*Change your thoughts and you
change your world.*

—Norman Vincent Peale

*When an archer misses the mark, he
turns and looks for the fault within
himself. Failure to hit the bull's-eye
is never the fault of the target. To
improve your aim—improve yourself.*

—Arland

WELCOME

 $\mathbf{H}$i! Welcome to this short book—this experience. It really isn't a book. It's a conversation. More important, it's a pick-me-up. It is a conversation between the two of us. It's a collection of questions, things to consider, and something I truly hope you enjoy reading. It also has large, fun print.

The reason for writing this conversation is simple. I have been very fortunate to find some answers, and, more important, to find lots of questions that no one ever talked about when I was a student in school—when I was supposed to be learning. This is what I want to share with you by writing this conversation. This conversation has been a joy to compose. It has helped me learn a lot. However bizarre it may sound, I have learned more since I graduated from that place called "school" than I ever did when I was actually categorized as "a student." Maybe the reason is now I am learning about things I truly enjoy. I'm also asking more general questions about life.

I am a teacher of sorts. My career is helping students (young and old) discover themselves. I share information with people across the country as a speaker. My purpose is simple—to let people know they are GOOD! Somewhere along the way people forget to just tell you that you are good. We spend too much time focusing on the parts of ourselves we need to improve or correct. The insecurities, doubts, dreams and questions you have are wonderful! They are your very own. Many people are so busy trying to find answers, but have forgotten to ask any questions. They don't know why or what they are searching. Unfortunately, we are not encouraged to question things. In fact, we're extremely curious little creatures when we enter "the school," but for some strange reason we're transformed from question-searchers to answer-givers. The simple fact that you have taken the time to open this book makes you different. I think it is very "wise" to ask lots of "why's."

Let me be very frank before we start. This book is just a collection of different situations, questions and ideas I want to share with others. Hopefully, others will share their own questions and ideas with me when they have read this book—this conversation.

Let's have a great conversation. Maybe not verbally, but at least a tremendous mental conversation. Through this short conversation I want us to be very honest with one another. I don't lecture. I question, let my mind debate and listen. It's safer for me to listen, and I usually learn a lot more.

This conversation is called "Who I Am Depends On Me!" It is full of my attempts to share my view of the world (which incidentally is a very positive world). Maybe you will be a little confused by what you read. I hope you are. In fact, if you spend some time thinking (thinking = debating in your mind) you might make some new discoveries. Thinking (questioning and debating) why we act, feel and think the way we do helps us decide how we will act, feel and think. Thinking for ourselves and the individual we want to be makes us take responsibility for ourselves.

This is your property—your book—our conversation. We both have an important role in making this work. If you feel the need, scribble in the book. If you don't like something I say, cross it out. It's your choice. If you want to cheer about something you agree with, highlight the statement, put a star beside it, or color it bright purple. What I am asking you to do is be selective. Don't accept everything I say as being the truth. This is written from my perspective of the world, which may be very different from yours. You are an independent thinker and have the right to decide what you will accept and what you will reject. I respect that, as I respect you.

Enough of my explanation. I think you understand. Let's talk . . .

Far away there in the sunshine are my highest aspirations. I may not reach them, but I can look up and see their beauty, believe in them and try to follow where they lead.

—Louisa May Alcott

The greatest thing in this world is not so much where we are, but in what direction we are moving.

—Oliver Wendell Holmes

Standards of Excellence

Not everyone says "Here is a list of what I believe" or "This is what I value." Whatever people say they believe, we learn what they truly believe by watching them. Regardless of what we say, our actions tell our true beliefs to the world. The quote by Emerson "Who you are speaks so loudly I can't hear what you're saying" is very true. The words "Practice what you preach" remind us of this fact. As does "Stand for something or you will fall for anything."

Years ago I discovered several books preaching goal setting. The books kept telling me I had to set goals to get anywhere, I had to have some specific, ultimate goal to direct me. Picking this ONE goal to direct my life was very confusing. The world is an extremely overwhelming place. How was I supposed to pick the one thing I wanted to do from the smorgasbord of the world's possibilities?

I believe the books (or authors) are correct. You move in the direction you are focusing. But I didn't want to pick ONE goal and end up somewhere only to change my mind later. Instead of pinpointing a specific occupation or location to strive to achieve (like so many of the people in the examples of the books), I committed to some general principles. I wasn't certain what I wanted to be "as I grew up," but I could at least decide the general direction.

There were lots of folks I considered successful, both inside and out. People who seemed to be living the type of positive life I believed I wanted to live. From all of these people I saw some common attitudes or beliefs that seemed to move them in positive directions. These common attitudes or beliefs have become my "Standards of Excellence." These are my over-all goals or objectives. Whatever situation or circumstances surround me, these simple principles always give me some guidance and support to make a decision. Please let me share my "Standards of Excellence" with you.

The four principles of the "Standards of Excellence" are:

The Goodfinder

The Pooh Principle

Leader Time

Commitment

It is a funny thing about life; if you refuse to accept anything but the best, you very often get it.

—Somerset Maugham

The Goodfinder

Simply stated the Goodfinder principle is making a conscious decision to look for the good instead of the bad. The principle has been referred to as being a "Goodfinder," having a positive mental attitude (PMA), or simply deciding to be happy. I prefer the "Goodfinder" title (which I must tell you is credited to someone I believe is truly a success—Mr. Zig Ziglar). It is literally being a finder of good.

As a "student" enrolled in an educational institution, I was required to take those funny things called "tests" to determine the even funnier things called "grades" I earned. Unlike many people, I like to study and I really like tests. It's an opportunity to show how much I have learned and share it in a logical manner.

One class in particular required only two infamous tests—the "mid-term" and "final." There was a lot of information to learn for the first test. I studied like a mad woman and felt very confident with my performance. After taking the test I couldn't wait for the next class period to get it back. I was very excited.

The day arrived and my professor returned "the test." I was smiling from ear to ear until I looked down and saw this paper filled with enormous, ugly, red checks. All but two answers had dreadful red marks beside them. The test was a sea of red ink.

Immediately my abusive mental critic started making comments in my mind—*"Stupid!" "Dummy!" "What an idiot!" "How could you be such a twit!" "You should have studied harder."* I really wanted to cry.

I hadn't noticed the professor standing in front of the

class watching us. Nor had I noticed the rest of the class. I was too consumed in my test and how terrible I felt. Finally my professor began to speak. "Obviously you are all thinking about your test scores. You look somewhat perplexed . . . Congratulations on a marvelous job! (long pause) Perhaps I should clarify my grading system. All of the red marks on your exams are wonderful congratulations to you. These are correct responses. I highlight what you answer 'correctly.' I want to draw attention to your successes. You know what you don't do well. I want to draw attention to what you do well."

Wow, what a fabulous idea! Even though I first wanted to strangle him, this was a wonderful philosophy. He truly was a Goodfinder, making us aware of our successes.

Most of us know our personal weaknesses—the areas we need to improve. Highlighting and appreciating what we do well makes us feel good. When we feel good about ourselves we are in a positive state of mind. We have a healthy attitude. Being a Goodfinder is not ignoring the bad or negatives in our lives. It is deciding to first look for and recognize the good.

Goodfinder = Looking for and recognizing the good.

*No life is so hard that you can't
make it easier by the way
you take it.*

—Ellen Glasgow

*Most people are about as happy as
they make up their minds to be.*

—Abraham Lincoln

The Pooh Principle

To me, Winnie-the-Pooh is the greatest creature who ever lived. Yes, Winnie-the-Pooh is an alive, walking, breathing creature who will never die. Yes, I know he isn't real in the usual definition of "life." But he is alive for me and all those who have felt his magic. In fact, he teaches or lives one of the greatest principles which I call "The Pooh Principle."

Winnie-the-Pooh teaches us that we can't know or do everything. He frankly says, "I'm a bear with a very little brain." He tells us that he doesn't know everything. He isn't afraid to say to the world "I do not know everything." To me this is a wonderful thing to say. If more of us— human creatures—recognized that we really aren't so smart or know-it-alls, we would be wiser. Winnie isn't afraid to tell us he doesn't know everything.

Winnie not only tells us he doesn't know everything, but considers everyone else a resource. He says, "I'll ask Piglet . . . Rabbit . . . Owl . . . Christopher Robbin." He values others and knows he can learn from others. What a smart little bear. And what a spectacular attitude!

He also teaches me to take time to think. Winnie simply sits down when he is wondering about something and thinks, thinks, thinks. Too often I am too busy (or more honestly, I think or say I am too busy) to just take time to think. Winnie shows the importance of simply shutting down and sometimes turning off our world. We need to question and think about ourselves and our world.

So many of Pooh's friends call him a "silly bear." But is Pooh so silly, or just different? He is playful and certainly extraordinary. So maybe that is what makes him silly. Whatever others call Pooh (silly, strange, bizarre), he is and always will be a hero to me.

The Pooh Principle =   Knowing we don't have all the answers;
Valuing others; and
Taking time to think.

Dost thou love life? Then do not squander time, for that is the stuff life is made of.

—Benjamin Franklin

Leader Time

Oh no! You woke up five minutes after the alarm rang and you are going to be late for work. You hurriedly race around, but you are still late. Big deal. Or BIG DEAL!

Let's try some math with the five minutes or 300 seconds (5 minutes x 60 seconds). If you work with 10 other people and you are only five minutes late, you are really 50 minutes — or nearly one hour — late.

Fifty minutes? Yes, 50 minutes. You are robbing time, a precious resource from each of your co-workers. Five minutes from each of your 10 co-workers equals 50 minutes (5 minutes x 10 coworkers). Wow! You are really late.

If you aren't early, you are late. In fact, you're stealing. When you're late, your actions are telling others that their time is unimportant. Ugh! How very rude. And the more often you make people wait, the more you will be known as always being late and probably somewhat irresponsible.

Leader Time = Arriving a little early and being prepared.

If you're not early, you're late.

Make good habits and they will make you.

　　　　　　　　—Cousins

No matter how carefully you plan your goals they will never be more than pipe dreams unless you pursue them with gusto.

　　　　　　—W. Clement

Commitment

Have you ever seen someone's résumé that listed the individual as a member of zillions of organizations, clubs and associations? Were you impressed?

Right away it may look impressive, but a list doesn't tell you a lot of information. Anyone can pay dues to a club or organization or sign their name to the membership list. Big deal. That is not impressive. The quantity of groups we belong to isn't important. *What we provide as active members to the groups we belong is important.*

I used to think that belonging to a zillion organizations was impressive and made me feel important. But what value do we receive by simply being listed as a member of all those organizations? What type of commitment can we possibly have to all of those groups? Contrary to what some people may think, there are limits to the amount of energy we can contribute to the groups we belong.

When we join a group we should join for a reason. Not the fact that it will look good on our résumé or it is the "cool" or "in" group to belong. Organizations are created to provide a benefit or service to people with common goals. People who belong to a particular church of a particular denomination (Catholic, Buddhism, Jewish, Baptist, Lutheran) share a common spiritual belief. People who belong to professional groups share a common goal of learning and growing to be better professionals within that field. There is a reason for that group. Increasing or maximizing the group's membership may be a goal of the organization, but as individuals maximizing the number of groups we belong doesn't necessarily increase our benefits from the organizations.

Commitment as part of my "Standards of Excellence" means the decision to commit as much energy as possible to whatever I am involved. Rather than considering the number of groups I can join, it is more important for me to join a group that I can give value to and receive value from my membership. Ideally, commitment is a criterion. Before saying "yes" when a particular group asks me to join, first I ask myself, "Can I commit? Am I willing to commit the quality time to this group necessary to feel I am a valuable 'member' of the group?" If the answer to this question is "yes," then it is something I will become a part. If not, I will decline and say "no." This evaluation process allows me to be a real "member" to those groups I belong. Because of the commitment I feel to the group and its purpose, I will be a valuable member. The commitment standard also applies to our personal relationships. Are we committed to the relationships we have with others?

To better understand the commitment standard, con-sider all of the "hats" you might wear—brother, sister, son, daughter, mother, father, wife, husband, friend, niece, granddaughter, nephew, boyfriend, girlfriend, co-worker, etc. Each of these "hats" are part of your life and how you interact with others in the world. Before taking on new responsibilities, look at how committed you are to each of these "hats" or relationships. Are you too committed to a particular friend and not spending any quality time with a parent or brother? Are you satisfied with your attention to all of your relationships? If not what can you do to improve some of these relationships?

Commitment also means being present. Have you

ever been at an event—a meeting or a class—and found your body present but your mind kept wandering? It happens to most of us. It isn't fair to be somewhere and not devote your total focus and energy. Commitment is both a mental and physical process.

In this huge world there are limitless groups and relationships available to us. How do we decide what groups or relationships are healthy or desirable for us? Sometimes we simply accept new responsibilities and relationships without making any decisions, without first asking "Is this something I want in my life or not?" Commitment is what value you give to the people and associations you belong.

Commitment = Committing 100% to the responsibilities and relationships we accept.

THE ME I SEE,
IS THE ME
I WILL BE

The greatest discovery of my generation is that human beings, by changing the inner attitudes of their minds, can change the outer aspects of their lives . . . It is too bad that more people will not accept this tremendous discovery and begin living it.

—William James

THE ME I SEE, IS THE ME
I WILL BE

Please let me share a neat tidbit with you. I wrote this a long time ago when the world seemed very crazy. I think you will appreciate it. To feel the magic of the message, you may want to turn off the lights and light a candle or get out a flashlight. Try to create a real quiet, calm atmosphere where you can feel these words. I'll wait until you're ready.

****

Hi! I'm the person beside you. I'm the person behind you. I'm the person across the table. I'm the person across the room. I'm even inside you.

Yes, I've seen you. I've seen you smile. I've seen you laugh. I've seen you hesitate. I've even seen you cry.

It's strange that we haven't talked or shared. We have so much in common. I'm a lot like you.

You see I'm a little frightened also. It's hard to just be me.

Yes, I have friends. Yes, I have family. But in this huge world, I'm the only one—just me. And it's hard to just be me.

There are so many things I want to do. So many places to go . . . It's just, I don't know. What if things don't go well. If I

25

told people what I dream, what I see for me, they might laugh
or tell me I'm wrong.

Sometimes when I sit alone, I think really hard and picture
what I will be. In these pictures of my mind, I'm really good. I
always do what is right. And whatever I'm doing, I work with
all of my might. You see when I'm alone there are no doubts or
fears. It's just my mind—just me. I'm not frightened to see, all
that I know I can be, when it's just me.

But with others, it's so hard. You know we all want to fit
in. It's important that I be the person others like and want to be
around. I certainly don't want to let anyone down. But maybe,
just maybe, I'm letting someone important down—me.

Sometimes when I want to say something, I stop and wonder if I should. I don't like that feeling. I wonder if others think
that way. I think you've felt the same. But I don't know. We
really don't talk about these things, you know.

Who am I? I'm that flickering flame. The flame beside
you, behind you, across from you, and even inside you. You see
I'm alone right now, it's dark. It's safe to talk about this now.
Remember it's important to fit in. But in those times when I'm
alone and picture what I want, the flame burns bright. It's a
wonderful feeling and I know it's right. Do you feel that way?

Thank you for your time. I feel much better now that we
have talked. See how bright the flame is when we talk.

Let's help one another. You know you have grand expectations like me. Let's try to shine like we do when we're alone, in
those pictures of our minds. The person in my mind is the me I
want to be. Trying to change to always fit in, doesn't feel good,
it's not right—it's not me.

I'm going to try harder to do what's right, to do what's me.
I'll keep dreaming those pictures in my mind.

Can I make a promise to myself and to you? I know you

won't laugh, you're very kind. You're such a good listener and you make me feel good. You see I'm not afraid to let you see this flame.

My promise today and each day may be difficult, but I'll try. My promise is "THE ME I SEE, IS THE ME I WILL BE."

Thank you for listening. Thank you for your time.

******

I hope you liked that.

Take care of the means, and the end will take care of itself.

—Gandhi

Feeling sorry for yourself and your present condition, is not only a waste of energy but the worst habit you could possibly have.

—Dale Carnegie

WHY ISN'T MY WORLD WHAT I WANT IT TO BE?

- *Why don't I have more close friends?*
- *Why don't things turn out how I want?*
- *Why don't I get along with others?*

If the world and the people in it aren't treating you how you would like, maybe you are looking at the wrong side of the challenge. Maybe you are focusing on the external world rather than the internal world—your world. You are one very important component of the entire world. But in the giant sum of all the people in the world, you are a very tiny fraction. Yet, this is the only fraction you have the power and control to change. First you must start with yourself.

Many of us are extremely critical of how the world is treating us. Everyone else has more friends, more attention, more good grades, more fun, more money . . . Why don't I have more? . . . Don't I deserve more? . . . STOP!

All of these questions or complaints are about what we GET. This attitude is a very selfish perception of the world. I believe there is a basic equation for each of us . . .

GIVE = GET

The GIVE side of the equation is first because it naturally comes first. The size or true value of GIVE determines the other side of the equation – the GET. These two sides of the equation (GIVE and GET) may sometimes, or temporarily, be out of balance, but over an extended period of time the equation becomes equal.

What is this GIVE=GET?

The GIVE is the internal part of the equation. The GET is external. Since we can only influence ourselves and change internally, we only have control of the GIVE. Yet, repeatedly we feel we aren't getting what we deserve. We complain how unfair the world is treating us. We complain about the GET.

Let's look at some examples of how the equation works . . . In your physical education class the teacher may ask you and another person to be team captains. Your job is to select your teams by alternatively picking members of the class. Typically, you and the other team captain first select the most able athletes and your close friends. How do you think these remaining classmates feel after you have made most of your selections and only two or three of them remain? Unimportant? Incapable? Leftover? The message we give to these remaining classmates is "You are not very good" and/or "You are least wanted." After feeling this kind of insignificance do you think these last people selected to the team really care how the team performs? Probably not. You have given them very little value and you will probably get very little commitment.

Or have you ever had a teacher who made you feel very important? You may not have been getting the best grades in the class, but the teacher gave value to you. Even though you raised your hand and gave some incorrect answers, the teacher appreciated your attempt to answer. This teacher gave you a lot. As a result, you probably tried very hard to do well in this class. The teacher made the GIVE side of the equation big by giving you value. As a result, what you gave—the GET side of the teacher's equation—was also big. The teacher received more from you when he gave more to you.

The same is true for the student GIVE = GET equation. Students who commit themselves to studying and learning give more to their teachers and school. These students also get more from their teachers and school. The GIVE = GET equation is very powerful.

Unfortunately, the equation has the same powerful effect whether it's positive or negative. The student who asks questions of the teacher, finishes his homework, and studies for a test will get positive results because the GIVE part of the equation is a huge positive. However, the same equality of GIVE and GET occurs for the negative. The student who sleeps in the back of the class, doesn't pay attention, and talks while the teacher is lecturing is giving negative effort to the teacher. This student will probably get poor, low grades and discipline (i.e. detention) from the teacher. The GIVE part of the equation is a big negative so the GET will probably be a negative.

What are you dissatisfied with? What do you think you aren't getting? Rather than focusing on the GET side of the equation, consider the GIVE. You are the only thing in the world you can change. You can change other things as a result of your behavior, but first you must make the change in yourself. You are the only fraction of the world that you have total authority and responsibility to change.

The credit belongs to the man who is actually in the arena, who's face is marred by dust and sweat and blood; who strives valiantly; who errs and comes short again and again, who knows the great enthusiasms, the great devotions, and spends himself in a worthy cause; who at the best, knows the triumph of high achievement; and who, at the worst, if he fails, at least fails while daring greatly, so that his place shall never be with those cold and timid souls who know neither victory nor defeat.

–Theodore Roosevelt

A man should never be ashamed to own that he has been in the wrong, which is but saying in other words that he is wiser today than he was yesterday.

—Alexander Pope

Begin to be now what you will be hereafter.

—St. Jerome

WHY ARE YOU
WHO YOU ARE?

Have you ever considered why you think the way you do? In America we typically hold the knife in our right hand and fork in the left. We cut our meat, put the knife down, change the fork to the right hand and put a bite of meat into our mouth. In Europe they do not switch utensils from hand to hand like Americans. Instead, they keep the knife in the right hand and the fork in the left. And in the East they eat with little wooden sticks. I don't know where you live in America, but isn't it funny that you probably eat by changing the utensils back and forth? Why don't you keep them in the same hand throughout the meal? Or why don't you eat with little wooden sticks?

Consider some of the strange things Americans do automatically. When walking down a sidewalk and meeting another person, Americans usually move to the right to pass one another. Is that because we drive on the right hand side of the road with automobiles? When two people are married, they wear their wedding rings on their left "ring" finger. Why isn't the right pinky or the left thumb or another finger or even a toe used to wear wedding rings?

Why do we have things called Equal Employment Opportunities or Human Rights? Shouldn't we, like so many other societies of other nations, simply be thankful for the opportunities of employment? Our great nation protects us. Shouldn't we simply count our blessings of contributing to our national economy which provides us with so much?

These are all strange questions. Your responses or philosophies about these questions is the right response or philosophy from your point of view. However, if you asked people from other countries or even different American generations, you might receive a wide variety of responses.

Why so many points of view? . . .

Different responses are given because people have been exposed to different situations and environments. You probably cannot understand why some people stand in line to purchase simple necessities such as shoes, food or toilet paper. Yet, people from other nations (or even other American generations) may simply accept this as a normal way of life. It simply depends upon what you have been exposed to and have decided to be the normal way of life.

You have grown accustomed to coming home, turning on the television and having alternative programs to watch. On the other hand, your parents may vividly remember having to make selections from only one or two channels. And your grandparents or greatgrandparents remember when the family sat around the radio because there was no television. They did not feel they lacked something because they were unaware of this strange device—television. Like your grandparents and parents, you are exposed to circumstances which make your expectations very different from others.

In some nations of the world the primary objective of every person is to make certain they receive enough food to maintain a healthy body. You, on the other hand, have enough food to maintain your health (and more than likely, a great deal more than you really need). Searching for food is not your primary objective. You have grown to expect to be regularly nourished. You expect three meals a day and possibly a few snacks.

What does all this mean? All of us need to look at why we feel the way we do and how we have acquired these expectations. Anyone can go through their day, routinely perform the same tasks, and never realize why they do what they do.

Ask yourself why you shower, get dressed and eat breakfast in some particular order every day. Is it because your parents had the same routine and you patterned yourself after this routine? Is it the most effective way to prepare for your day? If it is, wonderful. If you don't know, simply ask "Why?" You may be surprised at the strange patterns and routines you have implemented as part of your daily behavior. You are probably unaware of many of your habits.

Take a few moments today to examine why you do the things you do. Ask yourself, "Why am I who I am?"

It is not an easy world to live in. It is not an easy world to be decent in. It is not an easy world to understand oneself in, nor to like oneself in. But it must be lived in, and in the living there is one person you absolutely have to be with.

—Jo Coudert

WHO ARE YOU?
YOU NUTTY THING!

No matter where you go, you always take one thing—yourself. You take the whole package of bones, blood, muscles, thoughts and feelings. Everything that is a part of you travels with you. But how well do you know this traveling companion?

Are you aware of what you are saying to yourself? Have you taken any time to really get to know you?

Unfortunately, we spend so much time observing and watching others that we don't examine ourselves. This is not simply a quick external or internal view. This is a look at the big picture. This is a look at everything about you.

When you are talking to yourself (either out loud or in your mind), do you say appreciative comments to yourself? Or, do you focus on all of the things you could do better?

Do you walk with posture that nonverbally says "I like myself?" Or, do you walk with slouched posture that says "I am not very enthusiastic about myself or the world?"

Do you greet others with friendly expressions? Or, do you forget to look into the faces of others?

Do you value what others say and feel? Or, do you

generally have an impression or judgment of others before they say anything?

Have you ever asked yourself any of these questions? Do you know who you are? . . . Do you care who you are?

The moral of the questions . . . *Invest your time to get acquainted with yourself.*

We're all in a nutty situation . . . All of us are like PEANUTS. Yes, peanuts! We all have shells. Some people have very big, tough shells and others very tiny, thin shells. The shells we wear sometimes protect us from hurt. Other times the shell hides us from possible opportunities.

Some people listen and accept what others say about them without considering the source or the situation. When they hear people say "dummy," "troublemaker," "bully," "loser," "lazy," "boring," "stupid," "idiot", they accept these labels. In fact, they accept and attach these labels onto their shells. They expect to fulfill the behavior of the words on their labels. The more labels they paste on and accept, the tougher the shell becomes. It's a tragedy, but some people in the world are literally lost in the negative labels they wear. These folks never get beyond the shell.

It's our challenge to crack through our shells. It's our purpose to discover what's inside. The shell can protect some people from undesirable situations, but more often it prohibits people. Prohibits people from enjoying the nourishing fruit inside. The shell doesn't provide nourishment. The fruit inside provides nourishment, but we have to learn to get beyond the shell. We have to have a desire to know who we are.

You're a nutty creature! You're one of a kind!

Wouldn't it be nice to say to the world, "Yes, I am my best friend!"

We need to be surrounded by close, supportive friends. If we don't know who we are, we are living with a stranger. Invest your time to get acquainted with yourself.

The essence of our effort to see that every child has a chance must be to assure each an equal opportunity, not to become equal, but to become different — to realize whatever unique potential of body, mind and spirit he or she possesses.

—Fischer

BE HAPPY YOU'RE DIFFERENT

Isn't it strange that even though most of us have 10 toes, two feet, two legs, two arms, two hands, ten fingers, a neck, a head, two ears, two eyes, a mouth and a nose, others can simply look at you and know your name? You do not have to walk into a room and announce that you are Amy Jones or Bill Johnson. People recognize you. They recognize you because you are different. It is a thrill to be different. We do not need to color our hair or change the way we talk. We already are different. How you walk, talk, sing, laugh, shoot a basketball or write a poem is your personal trademark. It's your personal identify!

Sure we all need to improve some parts of our mannerisms. If you have terrible posture, you should try to walk straight. If you have a very small vocabulary, you should try to increase it. And it is important when you get dressed in the morning to project a positive image of yourself and your attitude toward the world. But it breaks my heart when I see so many people, both young and old, always trying to change, adapting the mannerisms of others or mocking the latest superstar's clothes, trying to fit in. We should be happy that we are different and proud of our personal trademarks.

Don't you agree?

BE THE BEST OF WHATEVER YOU ARE!

If you can't be a pine on top of the hill,
Be a scrub in the valley — but be
The best little scrub by the side of the rill;
Be a bush if you can't be a tree.

If you can't be a bush be a bit of grass,
And some highway happier make;
If you can't be a muskie then just be a bass —
But the liveliest bass in the lake.

We can't all be captains, we've got to be crew,
There's something for all of us here.
There's bit work to do, and there's lesser to do,
And the task you must do is near.

If you can't be a highway then just be a trail,
If you can't be the sun be a star;
It isn't by size that you win or fail —
Be the best of whatever you are!

—Unknown

We are what we repeatedly do.
Excellence, then, is not an act
but a habit.

— Aristotle

WHY ARE THERE "TEACHER'S PETS?"

Have you ever noticed that typically the same people who were *teacher's pets* in first grade are still *teacher's pets* ten years later? Has that ever bothered you? Have you ever wondered why they are *pets*? It really isn't that hard to see why they are *pets*, or how they became *teacher's pets*.

Unfortunately, on the first day of school your teacher was evaluating how you were acting. She/He was watching if you finished your work before doing other things, if you played with other kids, how much you talked, and a zillion other things.

Take a moment to remember how you did act in first grade. Were you one of the first ones done with your work? Did you talk a lot with kids around you? Did you say "thank you" to the teacher?

Now remember how the *teacher's pet* acted. Was he/she diligent in their work? Did they do a marvelous job at a lot of activities? Just what did that person do to make them stand out in the teacher's mind?

The teacher's behavior toward that *pet* probably was not the result of a conscious decision. The teacher was just offering his/her approval to that student for their effort. But when the rest of the class saw the teacher always praising the one student—the *pet*—it probably made them jealous. What we didn't realize when we were that young, was the fact that the student—the *pet*—had earned the right for the praise. Whether they were the first to turn in their handwriting assignment or they were the quietest during a lesson, they behaved how the teacher wanted them to behave.

It isn't a huge mystery why there are *teacher's pets*. These students have just learned the way to get the most positive attention from teachers. As a result of their "good" behavior, they probably received better instructions or more time from the teacher.

Now in 10th grade, 11th grade, and even in some jobs, the same people who were *teacher's pets* in first grade are still *pets*. These students are not brilliant, and they won't necessarily be named "The Most Successful Individuals of the World." They have simply been programmed or learned that positive behavior results in them receiving positive, constructive attention from others. Some students or workers who are jealous of this may say things like, "Oh, she is always kissing the teacher's ___tt," or "He's such a *pet*." People often ridicule or make fun of the *pet*. Rather than change their behavior or understand why the *pet* receives attention, the jealous people just complain.

Don't make the same mistake that so many others in the world make. Some older folks in the world still make excuses for other people getting the better promotion or the better assignments at work. The reason for these good promotions and assignments is a direct result of the person's attitude and work. Not many people use first grade as an example, but the simple lessons taught in grade school are very important. The important first grade lesson: We

receive positive, constructive attention when we **do** positive, constructive things. Those who complain about *pets* and say the world is treating them bad are sadly mistaken. Instead, they are not treating or appreciating their present position with the respect it deserves. It is an internal, not external situation.

Let's look at another fun example of how important first grade, or any other grade, may have been to you . . .

Quickly think of the teachers that you really liked.

Now think of the grades or classes that you really enjoyed.

Are they the same?

Usually your two lists of classes/grades you liked and the teachers you really liked are the same. The reason again is simple. You enjoyed these particular teachers because they tapped into what inspired you. There may have been some positive and negative times, but you knew these teachers cared about you.

You may have even been disciplined by this teacher. At the time, you may have thought you hated the teacher for disciplining you. Now, years later you still remember this situation and the reason for it. The punishment was not important. The fact that you had disappointed your teacher was the biggest punishment. You wanted to do well for yourself and this teacher because you felt valuable in this class.

There may have been other times when you loved a teacher for praising, either privately or publicly, what you had done. The teacher noticed you and what you had contributed. The teacher made you feel important. You knew the teacher cared about you and what you did. And you really wanted to do your best to make the teacher proud of you. You probably received good grades in the classes you liked the best because you wanted to pay attention.

My intent is not to generalize the world from a first grader's point of view. But aren't you beginning to see that many of the things we just talked about are true?

If you have been jealous of others receiving attention, you can start making a few positive changes today. Don't expect everyone around to see a huge difference or applaud you for what you are doing. As a matter of fact, if you have been placed in the category of a "troublemaker," those around you may even laugh in amazement at your new sense of responsibility to your work. If you really want to make a difference and start changing things, don't expect everyone to be very enthusiastic about the change. After your next assignments with your new attitude, your teacher (unintentionally) may even be a little suspicious of your sudden improved work quality. Your family may even fall off their chairs when they discover how well you are performing.

Let's also be realistic. Even though you may begin to spend more time on your work and begin to pay attention, don't expect immediate success. If you have not been applying yourself to your full abilities, some of your internal mindworks may be a little lazy at first. It's a little like a squeaky door. People notice a squeaky door because of the noise it makes. To stop the annoying noise you oil the hinges. Even after oiling the hinges, the door still squeaks. You have to push and pull the door back and forth to make the oil seep into the hinge. Your work with a newly oiled attitude is the same.

Your first decision is to oil the door or commit to

applying yourself. Don't expect the squeak to disappear immediately. You still have to loosen the hinges of your mind and program yourself for your new decision. But if you truly want to make a change, I guarantee that the squeak will go away and your efforts will pay off. Just keep remembering your commitment to make a change in yourself and your work. It is your decision and no one else's to make for you. You are a human being with a phenomenal mind. You have the ability to create your own future.

Make the commitment to yourself.

Nothing happens by itself . . . It all will come your way, once you understand that you have to make it come your way, by your own exertions.

—Stein

The day you take complete responsibility for yourself, the day you stop making any excuses, that's the day you start to the top.

—O.J. Simpson

BRATTY PATTY

Have you ever been with people who assume you will act a particular way or be a certain "type" of person? And even though it isn't how you want to or usually act, you find yourself acting how they expect you to act?

I am the "baby" of my immediate family and also the "baby" of fifteen grandchildren, even though numerically my true age is in the thirty-year-old range. When I am with friends it is easy to just be the real "me." They don't know that I am the "baby" or "oldest" or "middle." They have just grown to know "me." But with my extended family (which incidentally is quite large with cousins, aunts, uncles, second-cousins, great-aunts, great-uncles, etc.), who I do not regularly see, I am continuously pushed into the role of "baby" — or more appropriate "Bratty Patty." I hate that "role" or "type" of person which I have tried very hard to grow out of in my social and professional life. Sometimes I even feel that these people have pre-written scripts which intentionally place me in this foreign, uncomfortable situation or role. Now, I know you might say that I am just suffering from paranoia. And you are probably right. But that is how they make me feel. Or more important, how **I let them make me feel**.

How do I change this situation?

- Maybe eliminating contact with these people who make me feel this way is the answer. But that isn't a solution, that is avoidance.

- Maybe facing the situation without any preconceived notions of it being "bad" or "uncomfortable" is the best solution.

We read and hear variations of the cliche "you get out of life, what you expect." Maybe I am just repeatedly expecting these people to expect me to act a certain way or be a particular "type" of person.

(Wonder. Wonder. Ponder. Ponder.)

The next time I am in these situations I am not going to preplay dreadful scenarios of disastrous conversations or encounters. Instead, I am going to be bold, showing the optimism I share with everyone else who is not a member of my family. This is the healthiest attitude to have, and more than likely will have the best results. Next time I am just going to look forward to spending time with relatives and focusing on learning about their lives, not worrying about how I am going to act with them.

NO ONE SHOULD DECIDE THE ME I WILL BE, BUT ME. I guess that is a written pledge that I feel comfortable vowing to you. After all, you don't expect me to be any certain "type" of person.

We can do only what we think we can do. We can be only what we think we can be. We can have only what we think we can have. What we do, what we are, what we have, all depend upon what we think.

— Collier

The purpose of life is a life of purpose.

— Byrne

SHE DIDN'T KNOW
WHO SHE WAS

She was generally a happy girl. At least everyone thought she was happy. After all she was talented in many ways. But deep down in her heart where no one else could ever see or feel how she felt, she wasn't really happy. Everyone told her she was a "cute" kid and her teacher's praised her because she was a "good" student. People praised all the things she "did," but that really wasn't the important part.

She never felt complete, or whole. There was something missing.

Her family was what others considered "good." Both her mom and dad were liked by others and they never physically hurt her. And they never denied her to do things she really wanted to do. She took swimming lessons, piano lessons, tumbling lessons and many other lessons that kids take. As a matter of fact, she was always one of the "better" learners or participants in these classes. Learning was pretty simple. But she thought there should be more.

She never felt complete, or whole. There was something missing.

When she was in second grade she used to page through the Montgomery Ward catalog looking at the furniture section trying to decide which furniture she should buy to start an ice cream parlor in her basement. And after she decided the ice cream parlor really wouldn't work, she wondered if there was a way to sell houses in the neighborhood from her basement. When she decided that there really wasn't a market or a way to sell houses she found another opportunity. She bought packaged candies at the drug store, broke open the packaging and sold the individual candy pieces for a profit to the neighborhood kids. [Incidentally, she never considered opening a lemonade stand because that was too ordinary. The other kids thought of those kind of things. She wanted to do something different.]

But, she never felt complete, or whole. There was something missing.

She slowly got older and began participating in different activities. Her friends started to become a more important part of her life. She was in nearly every school activity and really became a well-known student in the community. She loved planning things and getting everyone involved. She loved the challenge of making things very professional.

But she never felt complete, or whole. There was something missing.

People began calling her a "leader," but she really never knew what "leader" meant. She was the same person she always had been, why were they calling or labeling her differently. Couldn't people see she was the same person? After a while, whenever she was involved in a group situation, people looked to her for guidance and advice. It was as if she automatically had answers to questions. Sometimes she felt very uncomfortable with these expectations others seemed to place on her. She was the same person, but the world had seemed to cloud or become confusing to her. It wasn't okay to just be a participant, she had to be that "leader" word. It was expected that she would accept responsibility and make things happen, and sometimes these were pretty "big" things.

Inside she often wondered if she had never gotten involved in activities how her life would be different. How her thoughts would be different. How her dreams and expectations for herself would be different. Life had progressively become complicated. If she was feeling a lot of stress at age sixteen, would she inevitably die of a heart attack at an early age? Yes, she did wonder that thought many times. But if everyone else thinks or assumes you can handle a million responsibilities, somehow you at least appear to cope with the challenge. But she wondered if she really was coping, or simply acting.

She never felt complete, or whole. There was something missing.

As she got older she talked more with her family at home, but they talked about the "things" she was doing, not about her. Things were basically the same. She still felt empty. There were so many things she didn't understand and so many things she wanted to ask. But somehow she had been discouraged or led to believe that these were the things you shouldn't talk about. Like . . . If your mom and dad are supposed to have a good marriage and really love each other, why don't they kiss or ever hug to just appreciate one another? Or if your parents really love you, why don't they squeeze you really tight and tell you? Is it embarrassing for them to admit such a wonderful thing? Why are things in family situations so competitive?

Shouldn't we just be happy when someone does well? And, why does my mom talk more to the dog than to my dad? Why? Why? Why?

She never felt complete, or whole. There was something missing.

Everyone thought she was satisfied and very successful for her age. But she didn't know what "successful" was. She kept getting involved in more and more activities and accepting more responsibilities. Why? She really didn't know. Some of the things she did she really didn't even care about, but she did them anyway because people asked her to be a part. This continued for years. Life kept getting cloudier and cloudier. There weren't opportunities anymore, just a sea of endless responsibilities. She was drowning inside, but no one ever noticed. After all she was a "strong" person, or so they said.

She never felt complete, or whole. There was something missing.

It wasn't until she was an adult that she, thanks to a friend, had a revelation. She finally saw things in a different light. A friend simply said to her, "You've done so many things . . . But what do you have?" She shrugged her shoulders because she really didn't have an answer. But she thought about this strange question for a long time. What did she have?

She realized that she had herself and only herself. Not in a bad way, but in the best way. She saw for the first time in twenty-two years that she was a person with emotions, passions, beliefs, and most important a mind. This is what she was and is. She was the same person she always had been, but with a better understanding of what she could do. All those years of devotion to outside activities and responsibilities had not really changed what she had been, they just brought them out. But why hadn't anyone ever told her that she was simply "good," that the "things" weren't what made her "good?" All those years of chasing and working to find something, something she always had—herself.

She had learned an incredible lesson. People grow by letting parts of themselves shine and by exercising these parts. She always had the ability, she just needed to let them shine. No one told her that she didn't need to prove herself, that people would appreciate the person she was, and if she didn't do a zillion things, it was okay. She would still be a "good" person.

She is still learning about herself, but she appreciates who she is. The "good" person she is.

You may think she is a strange and single instance of someone chasing for something, but people like her are found everywhere. If someone had only told her she was "good" and "okay" she would have saved a lot of time and frustration. The many things she did were positive, and she learned from all of these responsibilities. But the "things" weren't important, "she" was important.

At least she was fortunate to discover what she had been doing before it was too late—before she died. She realized what she had searching for all of those years she already had—herself.

RESOLVE

No one will ever get out of this world alive.

RESOLVE therefore in the year to come to maintain a sense of values.

Take care of yourself. Good health is everyone's major source of wealth. Without it, happiness is almost impossible.

RESOLVE to be cheerful and helpful. People will repay you in kind. Avoid angry, abrasive persons. They are generally vengeful. Avoid zealots. They are generally humorless.

RESOLVE to listen more and to talk less. No one ever learns anything by talking. Be chary of giving advice. Wise men don't need it, and fools won't heed it.

RESOLVE to be tender with the young, compassionate with the aged, sympathetic with the striving, and tolerant of the weak and the wrong.

Sometime in life you will have been all of these. Do not equate money with success. There are many successful money-makers who are miserable failures as human beings. What counts most about success is how one achieves it.

RESOLVE to love next year someone you didn't love this year. Love is the most enriching ingredient of life.

—Walter Scott

The difference between ordinary and extraordinary is that little extra.

—Anonymous

WHAT IS "AVERAGE?"

I have a strange question to ask . . . Have you ever met an "average" man (or woman)? Who is this person? What do they look like? Where did they come from? Is there some place called "Average Land?"

People have pet peeves, and this is one of mine. Some brilliantly educated individual probably thought this was a wonderful way to express statistics, but it is extremely irritating. Whenever I read little excerpts in magazines of some study, there is usually a category of the "average person." Well, often I fall into that category, and refuse to accept this awful label. I know I belong in the "special" category!

Has anyone ever asked you to compare an automobile to a tree? Or to compare a trash can to your hair color? Of course not. How absurd! But isn't that what people do when they compare people? How can we compare you to me. You may have had enormous challenges in your family life. Or I may have had a terrible physical handicap. Or you may have a beautiful singing voice, and I sound like a toad. We can't compare ourselves because we are so different.

Each person is like a symphony. All of our talents, skills, achievements, dreams, desires and passions represent the musical instruments in an orchestra. To truly make a beautiful sound we need to amplify some of our talents and skills at one time and quiet them at others. The degree of precision that we are using these skills, talents, dreams, desires will determine how beautiful the sound we create. If we really want to make beautiful music and achieve the greatest sound, we need to learn what works best for us. When the sound is not precisely what we would like (I mean if we aren't acting or performing how we would like), we need to make adjustments in our skills and talents. Regardless of how you use your skills, talents, achievements, desires, dreams and passions, your music is your own. The music I make with my talents and skills will never be the same as yours. No matter how hard I try to duplicate what you are doing, saying or displaying, I cannot be exactly like you. But I can learn from you. We all can learn from one another. We learn from what others are doing to make such beautiful music or how they are reaching their individual successes. Regardless of what we have as resources to begin, we all make our own music.

Let's talk about another type of average . . . The "average" grade in most schools is a "C." Well, don't buy that garbage someone may have told you long ago. It may be an average grade or it may not. It all depends upon you.

School is not difficult for everyone. In fact, some people receive great grades, but do not push themselves to the limits of their personal abilities. Some parents are great at helping their kids learn basics at a very young age. [You may disagree, which is fine, but I believe positive home environments and conversations help make school easier for some students.] But the "A's" received in school by those who don't push themselves to their potential are average grades for them. It is a shame they receive these "good" grades as a reflection of their so-called performance when you compare what they actually do to what they are capable of doing. I am not discrediting any grading systems. We need some type of grading system. The important thing we need to remember is our personal abilities or potential. How we personally compare what we could achieve to the grades we actually earn is the standard we should grade ourselves. Let me repeat this with a little more emphasis: How we PERSONALLY compare what we COULD achieve to the grades we ACTUALLY earn is the standard we should grade OURSELVES.

Consider the grades you receive and forget the little description of those grades listed on your report card (or if you are employed, on your performance appraisal). If you are truly doing your best, applying all of your talents and learning enormous amounts of material at school, you may still be performing well. Even though you may be earning "C's," this may be outstanding work for you. But don't be satisfied with those grades. Those "A's" do matter.

Don't let anyone tell you that grades are not important. If you are now earning "C's" you do have the potential to earn "A's," if you continue to want to learn like the "student" we'll talk about later. (There are many "students" who aren't in school, but are still eager to learn and curious about the world.)

Last time you got your report card (or performance appraisal) and you were either talking about it at home or with friends, what was the typical conversation? When your mother or a friend asked you "What did you get in English?" Did you reply, "Mr. Jones gave me a B–?" Now consider that reply. Is that true?

Grades are not given. Grades are earned and received. A more honest and appropriate response to your mother's or friend's question would be "I earned a B– in English." Now that is accepting your good grade and recognizing that it reflects your efforts in that class.

Have you ever heard anyone say "He (or she) is a B student?" Or "He's (or she's) a C student." Of course you have. It's a crime that we hear and accept these expectations of others. No one is a B student, C student, or any other kind of student that simply falls into a category. The "A," "B" or "C" adjective before "student" is not just a description, it often becomes an expectation for students, parents and teachers.

What grade level have some people placed you in? Or what grades or performance do you generally expect? Do you usually get those grades that you expect? Throw that nasty idea out of your mind. It may be stopping you from achieving the next level of grade or even two levels above what you expect. People usually get what they expect! Whether you typically get C's or A's, the principle is the same. We need to be more concerned with learning the information and performing to our best, than with that thing called a "grade."

Remember the last assignment you were given that you truly invested quality time and preparation. You listened attentively in class and did the homework assignments. Or at work you totally committed yourself to the project. When you really applied yourself and received that good grade or praise, whether it was A, B or C, you knew you had earned that grade. You worked hard for that grade. It was yours. That feeling of satisfaction and accomplishment was wonderful. [Please note that I listed

A, B, or C as the goods grades, not just A. If you truly worked hard and received a C for your hard work, you did your best and that is what matters.]

Now remember when you were not paying attention in class, or when you accepted the responsibility of a project with no commitment or enthusiasm. Remember when you did not study for that important test. Remember the low grade you earned for your lack of attention and commitment. There was not a sense of real accomplishment. You really did not want to own that low grade.

It's recess time . . . Please put your finger in the book on this page to mark your spot. [You know you want to keep reading.] Invest a little daydream time remembering those moments when you really felt a sense of accomplishment for your school or work achievements. Go ahead. I'll wait for you . . .

That may have been an extremely short recess or a long break. It doesn't matter. The key is to remember the feeling and energy when you did a wonderful job. You knew you had done well. Too often we concentrate or remember our poor or disappointing performances. We may think that by concentrating on what went wrong, it won't happen again. If you have not been paying attention in school or enthusiastically committed to your work responsibilities, you may have had to think back a few years or maybe when you attended another school or held another job. The key is to remember those great feelings and work for that same level of satisfaction.

Allow me to offer a small secret that may help you elevate that "average" label you may be wearing. You know you don't really like that label anyway. You know you are capable of more than simply what some call "average."

Keep those good moments fresh in your mind. Use them as energy for your next assignment. Do not even let a bad moment or feeling into your mind. By concentrating on the good and expecting the good, you will get better results if you truly apply yourself.

"Average" may be a comfortable label for some individuals, but I think you expect more than that. The grades you earn are important, but how you meet your own standards is even more important. Are you applying simply average effort? Or are you applying your maximum potential? Expect the best, work for the best, and that is what you will get.

Success is failure turned inside out,
The silver tint of the clouds of doubt,
And you never can tell how
close you are,
It may be near when it seems so far.
So stick to the fight when
you're hardest hit.
It's when things seem worse,
That you must not quit.

                                    —Unknown

Destiny is not a matter of chance; it is a matter of choice. It is not something to be waited for; but, rather something to be achieved.

—Bryan

The people who get on in this world are the people who get up and look for the circumstances they want, and, if they can't find them, make them.

—Shaw

OFFENSE AND DEFENSE . . . DO YOU HAVE A BALANCED GAME PLAN?

Consider the last time you and a group of people went to an unfamiliar location for a sporting event or activity without tickets or assigned seats . . . You probably walked into the stadium or facility and began searching for a comfortable place to sit down. Do you remember looking around at the people sitting in different areas of the facility? You may have inspected the clothing some of the people were wearing, noticed who was talking to whom, or the physical features of the males and females sitting in the area. All of these observations probably played a role in your decision of where to sit. You probably tried to sit by a group of others like yourselves. Right? The external image was very important. The clothes and attitudes you observed were important. It is strange how a group decides where to sit.

Allow me to share an experience with you . . .

I was invited to an evening reception with other speaking professionals and arrived a little early at the hotel banquet room for the party. The instant I walked into the room I felt that I was being inspected. [You know that feeling when you know you are being watched.] I noticed

69

several women across the room were watching or maybe even evaluating me. In a sense, they were delivering an on-site inspection of what I was made of simply by noticing what I was wearing and how I carried myself.

One woman in particular, dressed in a stunning dress with perfectly matched accessories, instantly gave me a hard stare and whispered something to the woman beside her. Instead of immediately becoming paranoid, I made it a personal challenge to meet this woman.

Later when the opportunity arose, I started talking to this woman. Our conversation lasted nearly one hour. We shared a lot of the same beliefs, hobbies and interests. It was a pleasure to learn about her. Before we finished talking I told her that I was very glad we had met. Strangely she replied, "When you first walked in I was trying to decide what type of training you were involved, and if you were with one of the host firms. I thought you were, but I was wrong. I hope to see you again. Good night."

The reason I share this example with you is to show you that the situations like the sporting event where you carefully select where you are going to sit based upon evaluating others happens in all types of situations. This experience of individuals evaluating and forming opinions of others with no real information happens a lot. Many people become conditioned to accept this evaluation process and never realize what they are doing. I truly hope the woman I met at the party considers how her first impressions can give wrong information.

Yes, we learn a lot from how neat an individual appears, how much they smile, or how straight their posture. But this is not enough information to truly know a person or have an opinion of them. We need to accept the challenge to make the offensive move.

If you are playing a sport—basketball, football—you may have a wonderful defense that really helps your game. Defense stops the other team from scoring, but the only way to score points and be the winner is with an offense.

The same is true for personal situations. We can build an invisible shell around ourselves and hide from the uncertainties of the world. Or, we can score points and feel like winners by welcoming the uncertainties of the world. Deciding to explore ourselves, others and the world is living offensively. For example, some of my personal plans of action to increase my offense with others are:

- start conversations
- don't be intimidated by the actions of others
- move out of my personal space.

These are ways to start scoring points and living for the offense of gaining points. If I had stayed within the confines of my own little space and not risked any possible uncomfortableness at the party, I would not have met anyone. The evening would probably have been boring. Rather than becoming victims of circumstances, we need to create opportunities.

Regardless of first impressions you develop, find out the truth. Opportunities are found in every situation. Don't rob yourself by not discovering them. By designing your offensive action you always feel an overwhelming sense of accomplishment when you meet new people.

Let's return to that sporting event. Don't play the defensive role. Be the initiator and the offensive player.

You want to meet new people and have a wonderful time. If it means sitting by some people you don't know, or being a little uncomfortable, sit down and accept the challenge of getting to know them. Cross the boundary that may be stopping you from having a great relationship with a new friend.

Please remember this: **No one can intimidate you.** You allow their actions, expressions, or your own insecurities to inhibit or intimidate you. It's your decision. You know you are capable of conversing and charming anyone you want. So try your own offensive game play!

Often people attempt to live their lives backwards; they try to have more things, or more money, in order to do more of what they want, so they will be happier. The way it actually works is the reverse. You must first be who you really are, then, do what you need to do, in order to have what you want.

– Young

GET PSYCHED!
MOTIVATE YOURSELF

You regularly see headlines and news stories about "motivation." Companies are always concerned with how they can motivate their employees to do more and increase their productivity. On Saturday morning after you have been lying around the house, you might say you have to motivate yourself and get something done. But, what is "motivation?"

Motivation is an internal force that gets you going. The commercialized individuals who claim they can *motivate* you are not using the correct verb. These individuals can *inspire* you, but they cannot *motivate* you. The word *motivation* is a derivative of the word *motive*. A motive is any idea, need, feeling or condition that impels to action; anything that prompts one to do something. Sure, an individual with a gun can make you do something, but you still make the ultimate decision to follow his orders. Motivation comes from within. You make decisions which lead you to a particular course of action.

The sportscasters often speak of great coaches such as Vince Lombardi as great motivators. These sportscasters are also using the wrong verb. These coaches were not great motivators, they were great at inspiring others. Their words, philosophy of life and actions inspired others to perform at their best. The players led by these coaches were inspired to practice harder and were dedicated to the team. These coaches used ways to inspire team members to motivate themselves. As your own coach you can do the same in your life. But how?

You need to find what motivates you. This may be extremely obvious or very complicated to determine. To understand how you can motivate yourself, try some of these personal inspirational techniques.

- Liven-up with positive music you select.
- Choose to spend time with positive people.
- Feed your mind positive reading material.
- Groom your mind as you groom your body.
- Visualize to prepare and expect the best.

These are just examples, not all of them are right for everyone. Choosing what you are going to do for yourself is the first step to motivate yourself. You make your own choice.

Liven-up with positive music you select.

Music can be a great inspiring force. Or it can be mental garbage. Do you know what you are listening to when you turn on the radio? Yes, there are songs with great lyrics and beats that immediately make you want to jump around the room and dance. These are great songs that make you feel alive. But when you turn on the radio you are subjected to whatever the disc jockey wants you to hear.

All of us have heard the music and crazy words of a commercial jingle. Somehow, even hours after hearing the tune, we still find ourselves humming that little jingle. This shows that our mind absorbs what it hears. Your mind does not forget the inputs you provide.

Be selective of the inputs you regularly provide your mind. If you feed your mind a regular diet of positive lyrics and melodies, it will produce positive results for you.

The key to working smarter is knowing the difference between motion and direction.

—Anonymous

Choose to spend time with positive people.

There are positive and negative people in this world. You have a choice of which people — positive or negative — you share your time. Make a conscious decision to surround yourself with positive people. This is a way to select what you let your mind absorb.

For years I didn't realize the effects others had on my thoughts. The people I associated with have always had a wide variety of philosophies and life behaviors. One day I heard a friend complaining and felt a terribly disappointed feeling inside. I was tired of hearing this individual always complain. He wasn't really complaining, he was whining. He was a very good student and was simply complaining about trivial things. I wanted to be his friend, but didn't want to hear all of this incredibly negative garbage. I had never really listened or analyzed the bulk of our conversations. After a week of considering this person's circumstances, I decided to confront him. I carefully told him that he was a good friend and person with so many things going right in his life that he didn't have much to complain about. Yes, I did hurt his feelings, but our friendship endured. Since this small event I have been careful to select with whom I spend my time.

We are subjected to countless external forces. Unfortunately, there are some people (like some teachers and bosses who may be negative) who we must spend time. But most of us don't realize that we do have a choice to make in selecting most of our surroundings. This includes the friends we regularly associate. Be choosey because you are worth it!

What the mind of man can conceive and believe, the mind of man can achieve.

—Napoleon Hill

Feed your mind positive
Reading material.

The last time you read the newspaper were most of the stories about bad things or negative situations in the world? The front page highlights horrible automobile accidents, a murder or a heated court battle.

You can make the decision to balance the material you read. Reading is great for increasing your vocabulary, your frame of reference and your retention level. Regardless of what you are doing or what future career moves you will make, reading undoubtedly helps you prepare. The newspaper keeps you abreast of current events and gives you wonderful conversation starters. It is important to understand what is happening in the world, but reading needs to be balanced.

Remember whatever you read your mind absorbs. As you read you are literally programming your mind. Reading at least a little sample of positive, inspirational material is a great suggestion. A "Books That Build" list is provided later in this book for you to start your own reading program. I am not forcing you to read these books, only trying to provide you with a little guidance. Once you go to the library or bookstore you will probably find more books that you will want to read. Reading positive material is a wonderful way to plant new seeds of thoughts in your mind and help you start thinking more positively.

Winning is not a sometime thing; it's an all time thing. You don't win once in a while, you don't do things right once in a while, you do them right all the time. Winning is a habit. Unfortunately, so is losing.

−V. Lombardi

Groom your mind as you groom your body.

As you prepare your body for the day you can also prepare your mind. Each of us spend anywhere from twenty minutes to an hour preparing our external bodies for the day. Unfortunately, the part of our bodies that really needs to be groomed and prepared usually doesn't get any attention. This part of your body is your mind. Try to dress your mind tomorrow as you dress your body.

Does this sound like an absurd idea!?! It shouldn't. It's a lot of fun and very easy to do. Simply remember all of the good moments of the previous day and how good they made you feel. Concentrating on these moments is an energizing experience. The feeling of success can be overwhelming and it can breed greater successes if you use it.

You may also have some favorite quotes which make you feel good. (This book is full of quotes with magical messages.) Write a favorite quote in big bold letters on a piece of paper and post it in the bathroom or on your dresser mirror. You will be amazed how good it feels to read and focus on this positive message.

Visualize to prepare and expect the best.

You may have an interview, test or important project happening soon. You can prepare for this important day by pre-playing it in your mind. This method is called "visualization." Let me explain how it works. . .

Whatever the situation, pre-play it in your mind as if it

were really happening. See the entire situation from your own eyes. If it is a speech, you see the individuals in the audience smiling and loving every word that comes out of your mouth. If it is a test, visualize yourself receiving the test and answering every question correctly. You may even invent possible questions in your mind and see your hand circling the correct answer. Follow the process to the very end when you receive the promotion or the test with an excellent grade.

Of course, you have to actually commit yourself and prepare for the project or test. Visualization doesn't do the studying or practicing for you, but it helps build your expectations and desire to succeed. If you set your mind to expect the best and realize any potential challenges that may occur along the way, you will be much more prepared to indeed have a success.

These are five ways I consciously motivate myself for greater successes. These are actions that inspire me. Try some of them. More than likely you will discover other ways to motivate yourself.

Best wishes to you in your motivational quest!!

Winner vs. Loser

The Winner—is always part of the
  answer;
The Loser—is always part of the
  problem;
The Winner—always has a program;
The Loser—always has an excuse;
The Winner—says "Let me do it for
  you;"
The Loser—says "That's not my job;"
The Winner—sees an answer for every
  problem;

The Loser—sees a problem for every
   answer;
The Winner—sees a green near every
   sand trap;
The Loser—sees two or three sand traps
   near every green;
The Winner—says, "It may be difficult
   but it's possible;"
The Loser—says, "It may be possible
   but it's too difficult."
Be a Winner!

Each problem has hidden in it an opportunity so powerful that it literally dwarfs the problem. The greatest success stories were created by people who recognized a problem and turned it in to an opportunity.

—Sugarman

IS IT JUST A "PROBLEM" OR YOUR "CHALLENGE?"

A plane bound for Miami, Florida leaves Chicago, Illinois headed north. Headed north? How does the plane reach the southern state of Florida?

It may seem difficult, but the pilot simply readjusts the instruments to make the plane turn and travel south. Consider what is accomplished by these simple adjustments of the instruments . . . It is quite awesome.

Many people have been faced with enormous challenges. Their lives seemed to be headed north when they wanted to head south. But they accepted these circumstances as "challenges" rather than simply life's circumstances that would remain constant.

Consider these simple adjustments . . .

MELVILLE BISSELL of Grand Rapids, Michigan was a china dealer who suffered allergic headaches. The dusty packing straw used in the china trade aggravated his condition. To overcome this aggravation he invented and patented a carpet sweeper to scoop up the dust. His inventive contribution formed the Bissell Carpet Sweeper Company.

A print shop worker of Lowell, Massachusetts, **HUM-PHREY O'SULLIVAN** suffered from cramped and tired legs. He started using small rubber mats to ease the pain caused by standing on the hard concrete floors. After fellow workers walked off with the rubber mats, O'Sullivan started nailing rubber patches on the bottom of his shoes. Once patented, the novel solution made O'Sullivan a very wealthy and comfortable man.

Rear Admiral **GRACE MURRAY HOPPER** was a pioneer in the computer industry. Hopper became very frustrated as she programmed the first computer which was 51 feet long, 8 feet high and 5 feet deep with the same, repetitive machine instructions for every software program. To overcome this time-consuming process, she revolutionized computer software by inventing the first computer "compiler."

HENRY D. PERKY, a victim of dyspepsia, lawyer and entrepreneur sought to develop a food that did not irritate his stomach. He began testing with wheat berry. The food grew in popularity and became a breakfast favorite. In 1930 the National Biscuit Company (Nabisco) bought the company which produced shredded wheat.

These people were faced with challenges. They made a difference for themselves and others by positively meeting these personal challenges.

Your challenges may not be as dramatic, but they are very important. Identify some part of your life you want to improve and make it your personal challenge to make it better.

As I grow older I pay less attention to what men say. I just watch what they do.

—Andrew Carnegie

Your vision will become clear only when you can look into your own heart. Who looks outside, dreams; who looks inside, awakes.

—Jung

POSITIVE VS. NEGATIVE
DO YOU KNOW WHAT YOUR
ACTIONS ARE SAYING?

In school a friend casually made a comment to me which changed the way I see things. She said, "You know, I like to be around you. You make me see what I can be." Undoubtedly, that was the greatest compliment I have ever received. From that moment I have made an effort to state affirmative or positive statements to others. I have not always succeeded in this effort (sometimes my temper or emotions speak before my mind interrupts), but I always try to learn from every situation. Of course, sometimes we must offer constructive criticism, but that can still be accomplished in a positive way. In this pursuit to be a sender of positive statements, I created my black/white card.

I created my black/white tally card for improvement by simply cutting two pieces of construction paper, one white and the other black, and pasting them together. Carrying the black/white card with me became a habit. Throughout the day I concentrated and noticed the words and actions I was sending to others. Every time I said or did something positive I made a mark on the white side of the card. When I made a negative comment or possibly a negative non-verbal display of actions, I regretfully placed a mark on the black side of the card.

As I said, this was my personal tally sheet or report card for a new objective. No one else knew what I was doing. This was just for me.

At first I was a little ashamed by the many marks on the black side of the card. But at least I was aware of what messages I was sending to the world. After days of tallying, I noticed a definite change. Soon the white side of the card began to have more and more marks and the black side less.

I was becoming aware of what I was doing and saying. Being positive may not have been my primary thought 24 hours a day, but it was a general goal. The card was my reminder. It was a great feeling. I was really getting to know myself.

I don't believe people try to spread negative words, attitudes and actions. We just don't realize the enormous effect our behavior has on others. We don't understand how we are acting with others. The black/white card can help you understand the messages you're sending.

Try your own black/white card. You don't have to tell others what you're doing. This is your personal tally sheet for your own benefit. You might be amazed how well you get to know yourself. It's fun to try new ideas and exercise total responsibility for ourselves and our actions.

AFFIRMATIONS

- I am a miracle that can never be repeated.
- I know who I am and where I am going.
- I was created with a purpose and I am a valuable person.
- I am full of energy.
- I am responsible for my actions.
- Love begins with me and I can give and receive love.
- I believe in myself.
- I am a strong and capable person.
- I deserve the best life has to offer.
- My self–discipline today will pay off tomorrow.
- I will let go of the unwise choices of the past.
- I am loving, kind, gentle and giving.
- I was good today. I will be better tomorrow.
- I have a sense of humor and can laugh at myself.
- I am loved for who I am.
- I am an open and caring person.
- I am a positive person and surround myself with positive people.
- I choose my attitude in every circumstance.
- I am responsible for my feelings and actions.
- I set the tone of a conversation with the tone of my voice.
- I expect success.
- I am no bigger than what it takes to upset me.
- I accept people for who they are.
- People need love the most when they are the most unlovable.
- I am big enough to forgive anything.
- Love is a decision and I have decided to love.

- I see the best in people.
- Every day in every way, I am getting better and better.
- I have peace and love in my heart and it radiates from me.

—Unknown

The pessimist sees the difficulty in every opportunity; the optimist the opportunity in every difficulty.

—Jacks

It is not how much we have, but how much we enjoy, that makes happiness.

—Charles Spurgeon

THE GARBAGE OF
THE WORLD

As I drove to work one morning I noticed the big garbage cans which lined a busy street. Obviously it was *pick-up day*. The day when the sanitation people visit our drives and haul away all the garbage we have created. I don't think we really think about our bags stuffed with cans, paper, leftover food, and a zillion other tidbits. Miraculously we put it outside and it disappears.

What about our other garbage? It's a pity we can't see our own personal, invisible garbage. The garbage we say and do. The happy smiles we show to the world, the laughs we make when we hear something funny, the nasty words we say to others when we are upset, the belittling comments we make to others, and every other thought, word and deed we produce. This is our personal garbage.

Just like the garbage on our drives which is sent out to the world, our personal garbage is also sent out to the world. Like the paper, glass and aluminum garbage, our *good* personal garbage—smiles, laughter, praising comments, helpful deeds—can be recycled. The good positive personal garbage is given to the world and used by others for greater personal energy. The multiplying power of laughter and the cause and effect it generates is tremendous. This positive, personal garbage is what we should be sending to the world!

But what about the other garbage on our drives—the plastics which are sent to dump sites and buried for hundreds of years. This is negative garbage which serves no purpose and only clutters the world, like the mean or belittling comments we give to others. These comments are negative and serve no purpose. They only clutter others' feelings, taking valuable space where other positive garbage—smiles, laughter—could be placed.

The world is learning the importance of recycling the garbage we place on our drives. Shouldn't we be much more concerned with the personal garbage we are giving to the world?

Listen to yourself. . . What kind of garbage are you sending to others in the world?

Can your personal garbage be recycled to help others?

We're in science fiction now. Whoever controls the media—the images—controls the culture.

—Allen Ginsberg

WHY BE A TELEVISION VEGETABLE?

Do you immediately turn on the television when you walk into a room? Do you even think about it? Do you make the decision to have the TV on? Or is it simply a habit?

Having the television turned on was my habit—or addiction. It took a lot of effort to kick the TV habit.

My change of habit happened after reading this little quote by Benjamin Franklin "Dost thou love life? Then do not squander time, for that is the stuff life is made of." After reading the quote I questioned how I spent my time, or more precise, how I was spending my life. I logged my activities for one month. The log showed the amount of time I invested in activities. To my surprise enormous amounts of time were spent (spent, not invested) watching, listening or simply sitting in front of the TV. As a matter of fact, my log had about two and three-quarter hours of TV each day. UGH! That is over 19 hours every week and 77 hours every month virtually doing nothing. With the exception of eight hours of sleep each day (but often much less), my available productive hours per week are about 112 hours. Simply stated, I was wasting more than half of one week each month on useless television. This disgusting realization told me something had to be done! I personally outlawed television.

The first few days were horrible. I admit, I was an addict! The annoying house sounds which I had never heard were amazingly loud. My fan makes a funny hum or more of a moan after the first half hour. I never realized how loud silence can be. At the end of the first night I had really accomplished a lot. Not necessarily big tasks, but little things that I had on my "I need to do this someday" list.

Many studies document that it takes less than a month to form a habit. Well it took less than ten days to truly break the TV habit.

It may sound crazy, but I am really proud of myself. Yes, I still watch television, but as an entertainment device, not just for the habit of the murmur of noise. And to be totally honest every few months I have a "video binge" which is a real treat. A "video binge" is carefully selecting three or four great videos at the video rental store, buying some great munchies, and enjoying an afternoon on the couch being entertained. This is a fun, relaxing way to selectively lounge.

Please don't call me a hypocrite. This "video binge" is a conscious decision to squander time when I choose. The chunks of time spent during a "video binge" are much smaller than the previous addicting habit. Eight hours of selectively squandering some time is much better than my previous programmed month of 77 hours of worthless audio-visual noise.

Take (or better yet, make) some time to find out how you invest your time. You may be surprised what you discover.

Turn on yourself by turning off the TV!

A CREED TO LIVE BY

Don't undermine your worth by comparing yourself with
others.
Don't set your goals by what others deem important.
Only you know what is best for you.
Don't take for granted the things closest to your heart.
Cling to them as you would your life,
for without them life is meaningless.
Don't let your life slip through your fingers
By living in the past or for the future.
By living your life one day at a time,
You live all the days of your life.
Don't give up when you still have something to give.
Nothing is really over . . . until the moment you stop
trying.
Don't be afraid to admit that you are less than perfect.
It is this fragile thread that binds us to each other.
Don't be afraid to encounter risks.
It is by taking chances that we learn how to be brave.
Don't shut love out of your life by saying that it is impossible
to find.
The quickest way to receive love is to give love;
The fastest way to lose love is to hold it too tightly;
And the best way to keep love is to give it wings.
Don't dismiss your dreams. To be without dreams is to be
without hope;
To be without hope is to be without purpose.

Don't run through life so fast that you forget
  Not only where you've been but also where you're
    going.
Life is not a race,
  But a journey to be savored each step of the way.

  —Unknown

WHY ARE STUDENTS NOT ONLY IN SCHOOL?

We learn simply by the exposure of living. Much that passes for education is not education at all but ritual. The fact is that we are being educated when we know it least.

—Gardner

The great aim of education is not knowledge but action.

—Spencer

Learning is not attained by chance, it must be sought for with ardor and attended to with diligence.

—Abigail Adams

WHY ARE STUDENTS NOT ONLY IN SCHOOL?

W e need to share an important definition. This may help you understand my sometimes out-of-the-ordinary vocabulary as you read. I believe student leadership is not just for some people who happen to be a particular age. Student leadership is for everyone. The Census Bureau may categorize you as a "student" because you are attending an educational institution, but are you truly a "student?"

My personal definition of "student" is very different from that of most people. A "student" is any individual *actively* pursuing knowledge. Maybe not in the school of Mathematics, English, or Biology, but just plain knowledge. Many so-called "students" I meet are in fact not "students." They are simply attending an institution—putting in their time. Some of the greatest "students" I meet are age 60 or more. They are not enrolled in a formal educational institution, or classified as a "student." These people lead the life of a "student"—eager to learn, grow and experience the world.

Try to recall your favorite teachers, or just folks you like to be around. These people make you feel important. They listen as well as share. I would propose that these folks who may even be older than you and supposedly

106

teachers of sorts, are also some of the greatest students. They are hungry for knowledge, trying to discover and experience new things. They are curious about what you have to say. Just because you may be younger in age doesn't make them think less of what you have to offer. These people are students because they strive to learn and realize everyone can teach them something.

So regardless of age, we all can learn more. Whether you are thirteen, thirty-three or eighty-three, ask yourself an important question, "Am I really a STUDENT?"

This book – this conversation – is for all STUDENTS, young and old.

We first make our habits, and then our habits make us.

—John Dryden

Nothing will make us so charitable and tender to the faults of others, as, by self—examination, thoroughly to know our own.

—Francois de S. Fenelon

SOME LESSONS WE NEVER OUTGROW!

Children hear, observe and absorb the world. Children learn from any source that sends information. As we grow older, many of us still recall some of our favorite children's stories. Unfortunately, for some strange reason, these stories, fables and tales don't seem so monumental as we grow older. I wonder why . . .

The lessons the stories teach are very simple and very important. We never outgrow these lessons of honesty and character. But as we grow older the world seems to grow more complicated. We're busy reading textbooks and newspapers telling us about the world. Sometimes the textbooks and newspapers make the world even more complicated to us. I propose the most undervalued lessons and reading material are those you read as a child. The messages are clear—be kind, take care of yourself, respect others. Maybe we need an overwhelming dose of simplicity to reaffirm what we truly value. Or once again discover what we value.

Why not indulge yourself and check out a copy of Aesop's Fables from the library? Or why not tune in to "Fairy Tale Theater" on PBS? Just because we have more birthdays and we are a little older, doesn't make us too important for these timeless classics.

Allow me to share some examples with you . . .

Rudolph-the-Red-Nose-Reindeer really is an admirable little reindeer. You know, "All of the other reindeer used to laugh and call him names. They never let poor Rudolph join in any reindeer games." The other reindeer were cruel to Rudolph, but Rudolph was not petty. He really valued serving others. When Santa asked him to help deliver toys, Rudolph could have felt sorry for himself and said, "No." But Rudolph wasn't vengeful. He showed the others that he was very strong. He won the respect of the other reindeer by helping when he was really needed. What a wonderful lesson Rudolph-the-Red-Nose-Reindeer teaches us!

Beatrix Potter created some of the most darling characters in her short stories. (Many Americans aren't familiar with Potter's work. If you haven't read her stories, find them at the library. They are wonderful treasures.) Her story of Tom Kitten explains how a mother kitten was preparing to have some friends over and wanted her kittens to be clean for the tea party. She washed the kittens and dressed them in their best clothes. She clearly told them not to get into trouble or dirt. While she was preparing food for her guests the kittens were busy playing outside. They got very dirty and lost their clothes. When mother kitten finds out she is very angry. The story shows that not everyone values the same things. The mother kitten valued her kittens clean appearance and wanted the kittens to be very clean for the company she had invited. The kittens did not value their appearance, they valued the outdoors and exploring. It is a wonderful lesson!

The Aesop Fable "The Hare and the Tortoise" is a classic. Obviously the hare could beat the tortoise in a race, because a hare is very fast and a tortoise is very slow. In the fable the slow tortoise wins the race. The hare is so certain he will win that he doesn't even try—he even sleeps. The hare teaches us to commit to our tasks and follow through on our responsibilities. No matter what our talents and innate abilities, we must try and commit ourselves to succeed. Another fabulous lesson!

We have heard the lessons and know the stories. But are we living the lessons? Are we living the principles we heard and were supposed to learn when we were children? Why not re-acquaint ourselves with these simple little treasures?

Libraries are full of treasures. They even have special reading or story-hours for parents to bring their children to the library to hear stories read to them. No, you don't have to be taken there by an adult. You can go yourself. You can bring the "student," (the "child" within you) to hear these magical messages. You can sit, listen and observe the magic of the stories on others and yourself. If the story-hour isn't the place for you, maybe you will simply browse the children's section at the library and pick out your own smorgasbord of lessons to enjoy.

We have heard the stories and the lessons, but we haven't outgrown them. It's a lot like studying for a test. We read the information or hear it from our teacher, but before the test we read our notes, study the book and review to make certain we know the information. The lessons of the stories and fables are the same. It is the information of life—what we were supposed to learn as small children. If we aren't truly applying these success principles—this elementary information—maybe we should rediscover it.

Some evening or maybe this weekend, journey through the children's section of your library. Even if you choose not to check out the juvenile titles, let yourself enjoy the memories of these classic stories.

Happy re-discovery!

*I am not ashamed to confess I am
ignorant of what I do not know.*

— Cicero

*One should, each day, try to hear a
little song, read a good poem, see a
fine picture, and if it is possible,
speak a few reasonable words.*

— Goethe

*We don't know one millionth of one
percent of anything.*

— Edison

Even Old Ideas Are Brand New

Everyone is born ignorant. We don't know anything when we are born. WOW, what a humbling thought!

We become little learning machines from the moment we see the world. The world is our laboratory. Even the most simple things like gravity have to be learned. Babies only learn about gravity after falling several times. Babies learn that a hot stove can be dangerous only after feeling the pain of a burn after touching the stove or being repeatedly warned of the potential danger. Babies are born ignorant. Since every human being has been a baby at some time in their life, we have all been ignorant.

In grade school we learn that two plus two equals four. What if someone your own age asked you today, "What does two plus two equal?" You might look at them oddly when you answer "four." This seems to be a simple question which everyone should know. However simple some questions seem, we need to remember that at one point in time we were all ignorant. We have all had different experiences and impressions shape how we see the world. We all have something new to share with other human beings. We all have something to offer.

I have been a student of positive thinking, self-esteem and leadership for years. Every new piece of information is another little light of inspiration which makes me want to learn more. In workshops and conferences I share this information with others and am constantly searching for new information. One day at the end of a workshop, a young woman walked toward me smiling. She looked very happy and started talking. "This was a great workshop and lots of fun. But of everything we shared, that little quote on the bottom of your handout really made me think. Thanks!" At the time I honestly could not recall what quote I had printed on the bottom of the handout. I looked at the bottom of the handout and saw the magical words by Emerson — *What lies behind us and what lies before us are tiny matters compared to what lies within us.* This quote has been a favorite of mine for years. It is found in all types of books and publications. To me it seems very old, but it was fresh and new to this woman. The magic of the message had touched another life.

It occurred to me that I should be very careful with the types of information I share with others. Even though some quotes and inspirational stories have been around for centuries, they are brand new to the person who hears them for the first time. The incredible words and stories from some of the great positive communicators — Emerson, Aristotle, Dr. Norman Vincent Peale, Og Mandino, Zig Ziglar, Denis Waitley — are timeless. Every day people read a quote, quip, story, comic that is shared by someone else. The information is not new to the person sharing the information, but it is a brand new idea to the person receiving the information. Every old idea is a brand new idea. Yes, every old idea is a brand new idea to the person who hears or sees it for the first time.

Allow me to offer a visual example of an old place

which every day is brand new. The Niagara Falls are a phenomenal beauty. Every day the Falls are an overwhelming site to individuals who visit them for the first time. Regardless of how many millions of people see the Falls, there are always others who have not seen them. Even though the Falls are very old, they are brand new to the individual who sees them for the first time.

Many of the quotations in this book are my all-time favorites. Most of them are very old, but they are brand new to you if you are reading them for the first time.

Just like the quotations, quips, stories, comics, or Niagara Falls, people can also be brand new. Every time we meet a stranger we are brand new to that person, and they are brand new to us. It is overwhelming to try to comprehend this enormous world and all of the people, places, ideas and experiences we have yet to learn. The simple pursuit or challenge of learning every day is exciting.

Knowing that every old idea is brand new to someone else makes me excited and hopeful. Excited to learn and grow and search for new information. Hopeful that those with information I do not know are eager and willing to share their wisdom with me.

Yes, even old ideas are brand new!

WHY ARE WE KILLERS?

The worst bankrupt in the world is the person who has lost his enthusiasm.

— Arnold

WHY ARE WE KILLERS?

We have human and spiritual laws that forbid us from killing others. These are easy laws to follow. Aren't they? I have never murdered another person. But maybe I am forgetting another kind of killing. What about . . .

the enthusiasm of a committee member that vanished when someone said her idea was bad?

the smile of the sister that turned to a frown when her brother laughed at her new brightly colored dress?

a husband's joy for a new promotion which disappeared when his wife did not congratulate him?

the new member's timidness which increased when no one asked for his comments?

the man on the street who cheerfully said "hello" and was passed with no return acknowledgement?

the young student who eagerly wanted to get involved but no one acknowledged his eagerness or abilities?

the professor who was surprised when his "average" student received an A+ and suspiciously returned the student's test without a word of praise or encouragement?

the mother who told her son it was all right that he failed arithmetic because it had also been hard for her?

the father who replied, "What a stupid question!" to his daughter?

the man who hurriedly relayed a terrible rumor about a neighbor to everyone he met?

These small events happen every day. Every day we kill one another. No, maybe not physically with guns and knives, but we kill. We kill enthusiasm, joy, zeal, excitement, and all those other cherished emotions.

Sharing multiplies our joys. Tearing down destroys.

*We must look at the lens through
which we see the world, as well as
the world we see, and that the lens
itself shapes how we interpret
the world.*

—Stephen Covey

WHY WE NEED TO
UNDERSTAND OTHERS?

We are all different. What makes you laugh might make me ill. What makes you angry might make me laugh. It's all a matter of perspective. Before we attempt to make someone else see what we mean, we first need to understand their perspective. The cliche attributed to the Indians, "You can't judge another until you've walked a mile in their shoes," explains the principle. Only by physically becoming another person can we truly understand this other person. Obviously, it is impossible to become someone else, but we can appreciate the background, philosophy, and circumstances of different people.

For example, in the action/adventure movie **Indiana Jones — The Last Crusade**, Indiana Jones shows us how important it is to understand others. At the end of the film Indiana Jones' father will die unless Indy can drink from what is supposed to be Christ's cup. There are many cups he must choose from. The villain of the film greedily drank from the wrong cup and died a horrible death before Indiana Jones. Indy carefully looks at his options and picks the cup he thinks is the right one. Most of the cups are incredibly ornate with beautiful detail. Indy selects a simple cup. Obviously as the Hollywood hero, Indiana Jones makes the right choice and saves his father. When he is asked why he chose that particular cup, he said he looked for the cup of the son of a carpenter. Wow! Indiana Jones selected the cup because he considered the other person—Christ, the son of a carpenter.

Like Indiana Jones, we need to first consider other people and what makes them tick. It isn't important what we think another person should want or act like.

We need to consider: *Where is this person from? What is this person's perspective of the world? In the very middle of their deepest thoughts, how does this person feel about himself and the world?*

You probably talk differently to your three-year-old cousin, than you do to your mother. This is a simple truth. But this principle goes deeper than the obvious difference between talking to your cousin and your mother. Even when we talk to people our own age we have to be aware of who they are. This other person is a unique collection of ideas, impressions, attitudes, and experiences. The way this person sees the world is different from your view.

By understanding others as different, unique creatures we might appreciate one another more. It may have a lot to do with our expectations. Indiana Jones understood the cup belonged to the son of a carpenter who later was named by some people in history as "The King," but this man did not begin as a king. Indiana Jones succeeded because he understood who this different person was.

The best captain does not plunge headlong
Nor is the best soldier a fellow hot to fight.
The greatest victor wins without a battle . . .

—Lao Tzu

Anger is a wind that blows out the lamp of the mind.

—Arab Proverb

THE CONFUSION OF CONFLICT

Remember the last time that you and a friend or family member disagreed. You had a heated argument and felt negative feelings. You felt bad that the disagreement (or result of different opinions) led to an argument. You and the other person or persons experienced a poorly handled or poorly managed conflict situation.

The mere mention of the word "conflict" usually makes us think of a heated argument, insults, or unfortunately, physical confrontations. But this is a misperception. Conflict is not the arguments, insults or wars we often think of when we hear the word. Conflict occurs when the expectations of one or more persons and the actions of another don't match. Conflict occurs at the moment when two forces don't agree. However, the portion we usually consider—the fighting, arguing, and insulting—is how we handle conflict. That is the portion that is often negative.

Conflict is not bad. Conflict just exists. It is the trademark that makes you different from me—different from all other creatures. Being an individual with your own knowledge, experiences, beliefs, passions and needs makes you a unique part of our complex world. Your individuality, which often is the source of conflict, is good. It is how we handle conflicting situations that is sometimes negative. This confusion between conflict and how it is handled needs to be understood.

The evening news often spotlights stories of countries at war. We hear the reporter discussing the conflict. The conflict may be two conflicting claims to a piece of land or the claims for the right of different types of governments to rule. Whatever the circumstances, the conflict is simply the differences between two groups. As we hear the newsreporter discussing the conflict, the visual images of the film clips usually show how the two groups are handling the conflict situation. Often times this is through the efforts of a physical confrontation—murdering, bombing, kidnapping, war. Sensationalized or not, the two messages we are hearing—the newsreporter's voice and the pictures of war—do not match. By not differentiating the two messages we begin to believe or perceive that conflict is war. But this is not true. The conflict is the opposing viewpoints. The method, sometimes war, is how the two groups are handling the conflict. The conflict may be good, but their methods—war—are negative.

It is our responsibility to start seeing conflict for what it really is. Conflict is a natural phenomena of life. It emphasizes the differences of individuals and groups.

Next time your mother asks you to clean your room or your spouse asks you to clean the garage and you don't want to clean, stop yourself before you say a single word. This is a common example of conflict. Someone else wants you to do something, you don't want to do. Their expectations and your actions are not going to match. Be thankful that you are different. But first consider how you will handle the conflict. Yelling and justifying why you are not going to clean is not the answer to a peaceable resolution.

Conflict is not a contest. It is our trademark of being a unique individual in this beautiful world.

Beware of no one more than of yourself; we carry our worst enemies within us.

—Charles Spurgeon

Everything that irritates us about others can lead us to an understanding of ourselves.

—Jung

He who gains a victory over other men is strong; but he who gains a victory over himself is all powerful.

—Lao—Tse

HURTING THOSE YOU LOVE THE MOST

Why do we often hurt the people we love the most? Do you sometimes feel irritable at home? Have you ever snapped back at your mother when she said something to you? You didn't even think how unfair and cruel it was. You just did it.

Years ago I was feeling really down for some reason. I don't know why. My mother was asking me to do something which I didn't want to do. Without thinking I was shouting at her. Somehow I just kept shouting. Then I saw her face with sad watery eyes. Her expression really hadn't changed, but her eyes were full of tears.

This is still one of the most horrible moments of my life. I felt like Satan itself. For no reason I had almost made her cry. The pathetic fact that the cause of the situation is forgotten shows how insignificant the cause must have been. But how I remember her sad face.

I didn't mean to be cruel. I don't think any of us mean to hurt those we love. Maybe we just don't take the extra energy to really safeguard the people we hold most dear. It is important to start practicing goodwill on our families — the closest people to us. Arriving home and not recognizing the special people in our lives is a terribly shallow habit. Is your brother in a really good mood? Is your wife extremely tired? Is your daughter preoccupied by something?

Interrogation isn't the answer. Simply noticing the way they are feeling and acting. Even if you don't say anything, your concern will be noticed and appreciated.

WHY DON'T OTHERS GET OTHERS GET INVOLVED?

To love what you do and feel that it matters — how could anything be more fun.

—Graham

The greatest ability is dependability.

—Curt Bergwall

WHY DON'T OTHERS GET INVOLVED?

"Yes, I joined that club at school. It's okay, but we need people to do things. No one wants to do anything."

No, everyone may not want to be part of your group. You may have a tremendous program and many successes, but some people don't want to belong. Why? . . .

All of us have different wants and needs and we join groups for different reasons. We join groups to satisfy some needs. The question we ask ourselves before joining a group (even though it may sound selfish) is "What's in it for me?" We may not say this out loud, but internally we ask this. If the question isn't answered, we don't see the purpose of being a member. If you want to get more people involved, let them know what's in it for them. In other words, you must find what will inspire these individuals to get involved. What will make these individuals want to be active contributors to your group?

Different people are inspired by different things. All of us like to feel that we are a part of something, but for different reasons.

Some people are motivated by power—the power to have influence or make a difference. This power is not necessarily positive or negative. These people simply want to have the authority to use decision-making skills and influence the group's course of action. If the leader simply orders people to do things, this may be a negative way to use her power. If she creates a system or environment where members can all share in decision-making and feel they make a difference, this is a positive use of power. If your group has a new member who seems to be power-motivated, you may appoint this member as a committee chair. Right away you are meeting this person's needs. You are providing an opportunity for this person to have some power if that is their need. Many people in leadership positions are power-motivated.

Other people are motivated by achievement. These individuals love to have a challenge. The greatest satisfaction to these members is to achieve a goal—to succeed. Often achievement-motivated individuals are first assigned small projects to complete. The more achievements the person meets, the more their needs are being satisfied.

Affiliation-motivation is another reason people join groups. Simply being with others and feeling a sense of belonging is important to the affiliation-motivated member. They need to know they are valued in the group. The fellowship a group provides may be the most satisfying reason for being a member to the affiliation-motivated individual.

Not all of us are motivated by one specific reason. We choose to motivate ourselves when we are inspired. The group has to inspire new members to want to get involved. If you are part of a group that is challenged by the lack of membership commitment, don't blame the members. Maybe the answer to the challenge is not the members, but more important what the group provides to the members. Is the organization providing opportunities for the members to contribute? Do members feel they are owners of the group's successes and setbacks? Yes, are the members owners of the group? Members must have an opportunity to contribute and feel committed to the group's purpose.

Any group can launch a massive recruitment or membership campaign to increase the number of members and collect dues. However, if the only recruitment campaign goal is to sign-up members, the group is cheating or short-changing itself. Before recruiting new members the group must first answer two questions: (1) What can we offer new members? (2) How will new members contribute? These are sometimes complicated questions to answer. The more time you invest answering these questions, the more the group will be ready to recruit active, contributing members.

If you're challenged by lack of member involvement, don't blame the members. First, look at what the group is providing to members. Second, how are members allowed to contribute and feel like owners of the group.

Remember: People support what they help to create.

A MESSAGE TO THE "LEADER"

Leader, if you want my loyalty, interest, and best efforts as a group member, you must take into account the fact that:

1. I need a SENSE OF BELONGING
   A. A feeling that no one objects to my presence.
   B. A feeling that I am sincerely welcome.
   C. A feeling that I am honestly needed for my total self, not just for my hands, my money, and my time.

2. I need to have a SHARE IN PLANNING THE GROUP GOALS. My need will be satisfied only when I feel that my ideas have had a fair hearing.

3. I need to feel that the GOALS ARE WITHIN REACH and that they make sense to me.

4. I need to feel that what I'm doing CONTRIBUTES TO HUMAN WELFARE — that its value extends beyond the group itself at some time.

5. I need to share in MAKING THE RULES OF THE GROUP — the rules by which together we shall live and work toward our goals.

6. I need to know in some clear detail just WHAT IS EXPECTED OF ME so that I can work confidently.

7. I need to have RESPONSIBILITIES THAT CHALLENGE, that are within the range of my abilities, and that contribute toward reaching our goals.

8. I need to SEE that PROGRESS is being made toward goals WE have set.

9. I need to be kept informed. WHAT I'M NOT UP ON, I MAY BE DOWN ON!

10. I need to have confidence in our leader . . . confidence based upon

ASSURANCE OF CONSISTENT FAIR TREATMENT, OF RECOGNITION WHEN IT IS DUE, AND TRUST THAT LOYALTY WILL BRING INCREASED SECURITY.

In brief, the situation in which I find myself must make sense to me regardless of how much sense it makes to the leader.

—Unknown

ARE YOU AN ACTIVE MEMBER?

Are you an active member,
    the kind that would be missed?
Or are you just contented
    that your name is on the list?

Do you attend the meeting,
    and mingle with the flock?
Or do you stay at home
    and criticize and knock?

Do you take an active part
    to help the work along.
Or are you satisfied
    to be the kind that just belongs?

Do you do your job well
    and without a kick?
Or do you leave the work to just a few
    and talk about the clique?

There's quite a program scheduled,
    that I'm sure you've heard about.
And 'twill be appreciated, too,
    if you will come help out.

Think this over, member
    you know right from wrong.
Are you an active member,
    or do you just belong?

—anonymous

These, then, are my last words to you: Be not afraid of life. Believe that life is worth living and your belief will help create the fact.

—William James

THE TINY, LONELY SPECK

Once there was a tiny, lonely speck of dust who lived in a giant room. Everyday the little speck watched the other specks happily playing in piles. The tiny speck watched the others roll together and move about the room. The tiny speck wanted more than anything to be a part of the other specks' fun. After all, it was very cold in the corner where the tiny speck lived all alone. The tiny speck just watched the others and waited to be asked to join.

Then one day the big man who lived in the giant room opened the tall glass window. Suddenly a giant breeze rushed through the window, picked up the tiny, lonely speck and flung him into the happy, playful pile.

The tiny speck was amazed! Soon he was laughing and rolling with the other specks. He was having sooooooo—much fun! The tiny speck played with the others for hours.

At the end of the day the tiny speck left the pile to rest. He wasn't used to so much exercise. He left the pile and returned to his tiny corner where he slept very soundly.

The very next day he woke up and wondered, "Should I join the others today?" Without hesitation he hopped into the pile. Again, he had a wonderful day.

Each day the tiny speck continued to play with the others. The tiny speck wasn't lonely anymore, and didn't feel very tiny either. Now he was very happy. The unexpected breeze made him a part of something which he loved more than anything—the others.

Nothing comes from doing nothing.

—Shakespeare

In the middle of difficulty lies opportunity.

—Einstein

WHY IS EVERYONE COMPLAINING ABOUT SCHOOL?

Magazines, newspapers and television continue telling us that American schools are awful. Everyone seems to be complaining about education. What are the complaints?

Schools need more money.
Teachers need to care more.
Students need to shape-up.
Parents have to get involved.
Society has to re-evaluate its priorities.

All of these may be justifiable complaints for some circumstances, but I am not going to waste your time talking about complaints. Instead of debating any part of this issue, I would like to defend, promote, and/or re-discover one hidden part of school. This part is very old, but often forgotten. This incredible resource is the groups/clubs/chapters in schools. Whether it is a judo, science, chess, business, honorary, or skiing club at a school, these incredible opportunities are being forgotten.

Rather than complaining about the "awful schools" I

would like to find some solutions. Solutions begin when we look at challenges differently. Here is a somewhat different look at schools . . .

I perceive schools to be small communities. Your school is very different from other schools, just like your community is different than other communities. Each class available to you is like a different store. You select which store you are going to spend your time. Depending upon the community (the school), you can visit anywhere from five to ten different stores/classes in one day. The number of students deciding to spend time in any one store often depends upon the teacher (or the store merchant). It is the merchant's/teacher's store. He decides what kind of window dressing he is going to use. He could market the store/class to be extremely alive with inviting experiments and activities. Or he may choose to stick to the basics and not offer much extra than the textbook and tests. How the merchant/teacher markets his store/class has a tremendous effect on how you behave when you are in this store/class.

The classroom is the presentation and application of facts. The teacher is the merchant with enormous amounts of information. You purchase the information from this merchant/teacher by paying attention and investing time studying. The merchant/teacher is aware of which shopper/student wants to pay attention to the information. Each shopper/student brings their attitude to the store/class with them every day. The positive attitude the shopper/student brings to the store/class makes the merchant/teacher give more information to the shopper/student. The merchant's/teacher's skill is identifying which shopper/student is ready for more information and/or who needs to be given more attention. The merchant/teacher has an overwhelming job.

What happens next for the shopper/student after they have visited the stores/classes? Do they simply go home and do a few assignments? Do the students all go to work to make some money? Is the presentation of facts in the stores/classes the only service this community offers to its residents/students?

In your community do people simply shop for what they want and then go home? Or do people interact in any other ways?

Of course, they interact. The opportunities to interact and learn more skills in our school communities are through groups — teams, clubs, and chapters. The classroom provides us information, knowledge and basic survival needs, but this is only part of the big picture. There is so much left for you to accomplish and experience. Extracurricular and co-curricular groups provide you with this extra opportunity, this advantage.

For example . . . Joe is enrolled in a keyboarding class. He is very frustrated by the teacher who is always asking the students to do these ridiculous drills to increase their speed and accuracy. But Joe is also a member of Student Council. He has accepted the responsibility to invite the mayor to speak at a Student Council banquet. Joe has to write a letter to the mayor. This small, simple task shows Joe the importance of his keyboarding and English class. The reason he is in these classes is understood.

Joan is enrolled in an accounting class and two math courses. She likes to work with numbers and earns very good grades in these classes. Joan is also in charge of planning the National Honor Society (NHS) dance. Part of this responsibility is to decide how NHS will pay for the dance. Her classes are important to teach her the basics of how the numbers work, but now Joan has a bigger challenge. She has to find the numbers she is going to use in her calculations. The numbers are not simply given to her by the textbook. This is a very important job. Joan is using her math and accounting knowledge in a real-world challenge.

Jean is enrolled in a family-living class which she enjoys. She is also a member of the volleyball team. The team has recently lost one of their starting setters who was hurt in practice. The team is faced with a big challenge in re-designing their offense without this one starter. Jean is using some of the skills she has learned in the family-living class to help empathize with some of the team members' frustrations and helping everyone understand that they have to make changes. She didn't realize how much the class discussions about time management and role-models would benefit her volleyball team's success.

These are just three examples of three different students—Joe, Joan and Jean—using their classroom information in real situations. When students get involved in the school community's groups the information they learn is better understood. The students see how they can use their knowledge.

Sure there are many ways we can improve our school communities. Students, parents, teachers, administrators, and society could all help change our schools. The classroom is only the starting point of learning information. The ways students get involved and use this information is extremely important. Students have to have an opportunity to see the value of the information they learn.

If you had one-dollar bills piled from your floor to ceiling and didn't know they had any value, what would you do? You could wallpaper your room with them. You could line your bird cage with them. You could use them as toilet paper. You could use them for lots of strange, ridiculous things. Until you learn these one-dollar bills have value to let you buy things, the bills mean nothing. Everything we have or learn has to have some value. Participating in school community groups is an opportunity to feel the value of all that you know.

A LEADER?

A LEADER?

It's extremely difficult to lead further than you have gone yourself.

Good leaders take a little more than their share of the blame, a little less than their share of the credit.

Leaders are those who have two characteristics: first, they are going somewhere; second, they are able to persuade other people to go with them.

Good leaders inspire others to have confidence in them; Great leaders inspire others to have confidence in themselves.

Leaders are ordinary people with extraordinary determination.

****

All these quotes are about leadership and leaders . . . who they are and what they do. Each statement says something a little different.

Do you agree with all of these statements? Is leadership necessarily one thing or another? Or is it something unique that we experience?

What is your definition of leadership? Who are the leaders in your life?

A WISH FOR LEADERS

I sincerely wish you will have the experience of thinking up a new idea, planning it, organizing it, and following it to completion and having it be magnificently successful. I also hope you'll go through the same process and have something "bomb out."

I wish you could know how it feels "to run" with all your heart and — lose horribly.

I wish that you could achieve some great good for mankind, but have nobody know about it except you.

I wish you could find something so worthwhile that you deem it worthy of investing your life.

I hope you become frustrated and challenged enough to begin to push back the barriers of your own personal limitations.

I hope you make a stupid, unethical mistake and get caught red-handed and are big enough to say those magic words, "I was wrong."

I hope you give so much of yourself that some days you wonder if it's worth it all.

I wish for you the worst kind of criticism for everything you do, because that makes you fight to achieve beyond what you normally would.

I wish for you the experience of leadership.

—Unknown

You possess a potent force that you either use, or misuse, hundreds of times every day.

—J. Martin Kohe

ARE LEADERS GOOD OR BAD? OR ARE LEADERS BOTH GOOD AND BAD?

Does a person have to be a positive force to be a leader?

Is a person with ulterior motives and a tremendous need to control others a leader?

I present a seminar entitled "Leader Perceptions" where I ask the participants to write down a *leader* and a few words or adjectives describing the traits/characteristics that make this person a *leader*. This *leader* can be a person, thing, group, fictitious, deceased, or living. The only criteria is that the *leader* represent leadership to the individual. These instructions are very vague because I don't want to stifle or direct the participants' own thoughts. Second, each individual shares their individual *leader* and adjectives with the rest of their team. After all team members share their *leader* and adjectives, the team selects a team *leader* and adjectives. Again, the *leader* can be a person, thing, group, fictitious, deceased, or living. . . whatever the team feels represents a "leader."

The discussion is usually quite loud when the teams are each selecting a *leader* and adjectives. Each team is then asked to have a member share the *leader* and adjectives they have selected. The range of team responses has been enormous . . . Bill Clinton, George Bush, Colin Powell, Michael Jordan, parents, Nelson Mandella, a special teacher. As the teams share their *leaders* and adjectives I write them on the board and finally share some of my own. For example, Winnie-the-Pooh for the lessons of the Pooh Principle and Barbara Walters for her personal touch and thorough preparation. The last item I write on the board in huge letters is HITLER and ask the participants, "Was this man a *leader?*" The participants usually have expressionless faces while their brains digest and debate this question. Some individuals say, "No, he was horrible. He was not a leader." Others say, "Maybe he was bad, but he was a leader." The debate continues and we all share what we feel. It is always a wonderful debate. "Does a person have to have positive motives or intentions to be considered a leader?" is the question we debate.

Try a personal example to help clarify the question. At some point in your life you probably have known a bully who tried to intimidate others. The bully often picked on people physically smaller or weaker than himself. The bully picked fights he/she could win. Now that makes sense. Bullies select their prey or victims—the people they will influence. The bully influences others to do what he/she wants. Using personal skills to get desired results could easily be part of a leadership definition. But the bully is usually considered *bad* or *mean* or *a creep*, not a *leader. Why isn't the bully considered a leader, or is he/she a leader?*

There are literally hundreds of definitions of leadership. Typically, the more definitions I read, the more confused I become. But one fact is very clear by the definitions. Different individuals perceive leadership differently.

- Is leadership the actual act of influencing someone?
- Is leadership an immediate skill or talent?
- Is leadership a group of ideas and talents individuals collect?
- Is leadership the lasting impact or impression someone leaves on another person?
- What is this thing called "leadership?"

My perception of leadership allows a leader to be both positive and/or negative. A leader (individual) has choices to either coerce someone to do something or persuade the individual to act. Coercive leadership is negative. Persuasive leadership is positive.

I believe leadership can be positive or negative, but prefer positive. As individuals, we look to leaders for guidance. Every individual has a responsibility to look for positive leadership. We must be certain to send a clear message that we desire and strive for positive leadership. We need leadership which not only helps us grow, but helps all individuals grow.

In America we have the luxury of debating this question because we live in a democracy. So many people of the world do not have this luxury. Many people are simply victims of coercive, negative leaders. We should be very thankful for our choices of leadership.

Does a person have to be a positive force to be a leader?

Is a person with ulterior motives and a tremendous need to control others a leader?

Hmmmm . . . What do you think?

THE LEADERS BLESSING

Blessed are they who believe in the organization they
  serve,
    for their work will have dedication.
Blessed are they who guide rather than dictate,
    for they shall have cooperation.
Blessed are they who respect the opinions of others,
    for they shall be admired.
Blessed are they who present their points tactfully,
    for they shall succeed.
Blessed are they who search out the facts and ignore the
  gossip,
    for they shall be respected.
Blessed are they who give credit to others, overcoming
  jealousy,
    for they shall have willing helpers.
Blessed are they who seek to be humble,
    for they have a due share of recognition without look-
      ing for it.
Blessed are they who can take orders as well as give them,
    for therein lies true leadership.
Blessed are they who in spite of criticism,
  have the strength of purpose to continue
  and the stamina to carry on,
    for they shall be real leaders.
Blessed are they who have faith in all their fellowmen,
    for they themselves are justified.

                                        —Unknown

VALUE . . .
AMERICA

The highest values are priceless.

—Anonymous

The things of greatest value in life
are those things that multiply when
divided.

—Anonymous

VALUE. . .AMERICA

Recently I went shopping. The first stop was the grocery store where I gave the cashier four $1 bills to pay for the items I purchased. The next stop was the department store. I gave the clerk a fifty-dollar bill to pay for a shirt.

No big deal. If we buy things we have to pay for them. Right?

These two transactions may not seem very odd, but on the drive home I wondered what was the real difference between the two purchases. At the first store I gave the clerk pieces of paper with "1" printed in each corner and George Washington's picture. At the second store I gave the clerk a similar piece of green paper, but this bill had "50" printed in each corner and Ulysses Grant's picture.

Was there a real difference between these two pieces of paper? Was Grant more important than Washington? Why wouldn't the department store clerk accept only one piece of paper with Washington's picture? Why does one bill have greater value than the other?

If you have a few bills in your wallet you might like to take them out. Look at them. Touch them. Crumple them. Look at the little fibers in each bill when you hold it up to the light. What pictures are on these bills? Have you ever really looked at these green bills you handle every day?

The materials used to manufacture the bills don't make them different. The value they represent is the real difference between the two bills. The $50 bill purchases more than the $1 bill.

Sure, it doesn't take a genius to figure that out. We learn to count money in grade school. But did you ever consider or question what makes the bills worth anything? Why will almost anyone on the face of the Earth accept U.S. dollars? These bills or dollars have enormous value.

With every purchase we show our value or faith in our government. Bills are printed on strange cloth-like paper and distributed by our government. We trust that the American government who prints the bills is a valuable asset. We must have enormous value in our government. Unfortunately, we make so many transactions that we forget to appreciate the real value of our dollars or what they truly represent . . .

The real value is the faith in America—the faith in ourselves.

*Work joyfully and peacefully,
knowing that right thoughts and right
efforts will inevitably bring about
right results.*

—James Allen

*You may live in an imperfect world
but the frontiers are not all closed
and the doors are not all shut.*

—Maxwell Maltz

WHAT IS LABOR DAY?

As Americans we celebrate Labor Day as a vacation day. We don't really celebrate "Labor" Day. For most of us it symbolizes the end of summer—the last hurrah for picnics. We don't consider why we have this great vacation day.

The real reason we have the day is to celebrate the achievements of the great labor movement. Those who fought to give workers a minimum wage, sick leaves without fear of losing a job, a 40-hour work week, benefits to care for families, and many other luxuries we now forget to appreciate.

Anyone who has ever read *The Jungle* (which I highly recommend) has felt the nausea from those brief pages describing dreadful labor conditions. These are the reasons why we should count our blessings and respect the wonderful labor situations we enjoy today.

Sure we celebrate the day and the labor of preparing a family picnic, but not the real "labor" the day celebrates. The labor of those special people who fought hard and organized themselves to ensure we (the workers of today) would not have to suffer as they did. Now we, the workers they fought for, don't even really (truly in our hearts) pay them respect or remembrance on that special day.

We complain or gripe about some bosses, working

conditions, or situations, but let's look at all of the wonderful things about our jobs. You know at the end of the week or the end of every other week you are going to receive a specific amount of pay for your labor. You also know what is expected of you within your typical 40-hour work week. And if you work longer you will be given overtime pay for your extra contributions. To me that sounds like satisfying labor.

Next Labor Day I am not going to simply say "adios" to the summer, but say "thank you" to some courageous folks. And tomorrow at work I'm going to have a very good day enjoying my benefits as an American worker.

WHY DOES AMERICA HAVE SO MANY NAMES?

I often wonder what people in other countries think about our country—America. I also wonder if they get confused simply remembering what to call our country. After all, we are **The United States of America** or just **America** or just **The United States** or sometimes just **The States** or sometimes just **The U.S.** or **The U.S.A.** or **The U.S. of A.** The proper or full name of our country is **The United States of America**, but with all of these slang names and variations I wonder how the textbooks and newspapers in other countries refer to our country.

After all, I get confused with Germany, Russia and what is/was the Soviet Union.

READING. . .
WONDERING. . .
WRITING

Man's mind, stretched to a new idea, never goes back to its original dimension.

—Oliver Wendell Holmes

BOOKS THAT BUILD

There is so much information to hear, share and discuss in the world. Libraries and bookstores are enormous valves bursting with information waiting for you. All you have to do is take one book from this valve of information and you begin the wonderful process of your own discovery. You begin to be inspired by the energizing words you read. It is an amazing feeling! The more you read, the more you discover. And the more you discover, the more you want to discover.

These enormous valves of information (libraries or bookstores) can also be intimidating. With so many choices, where do you start? To help you start this discovery I would like to share some inspiring books with you. Begin your first step of this information adventure with any one of these books.

The list is entitled "Books that Build" because each of these books has a powerful message that literally builds. The inspiring messages build your mind and attitude.

The purpose of the list is to provide you with some guidance. Once you find and read a few of these powerful messages, you will begin to understand why these books build. The trip to the library or bookstore will become an adventure to find new information. Remember the section of this book "Even Old Ideas Are Brand New." Some of these books are very old, but the messages are timeless.

The "Books That Build" list is divided into two sections. The first section includes books that are tremendous starting points. Most of the books in the first section deal with attitudes and perceptions. The second section includes books that go one step further and explain more specific and in-depth information. May I suggest starting with a book from the first section and later enjoying those from the second section. It's your decision. Whatever book you chose to read from the list, I hope you enjoy yourself. Each book is highly recommended because each is a BOOK THAT BUILDS!

Books That Build!

A Better Way to Live — Og Mandino
All I Really Need to Know I Learned in Kindergarten — Robert Fulghum
Chicken Soup for the Soul — Jack Canfield and Mark Victor Hansen
The Giving Tree — Shel Silverstein
Hope for the Flowers — Trina Paulus
How to be Your Own Best Friend — Newman & Berkowitz
Life 101 — Peter McWilliams
The Little Prince — Antoine de Saint Exupery
Mission: Success! — Og Mandino
The Power of Positive Thinking — Norman Vincent Peale
The Precious Present — Spencer Johnson

Psycho-Cybernetics — Maxwell Maltz
Psychology of Winning — Denis Waitley
See You at the Top — Zig Ziglar
Seeds of Greatness — Denis Waitley
Top Performance — Zig Ziglar

****

7 Habits of Highly Effective People — Stephen
    Covey
Are You Communicating? — Donald Walton
GMP Greatest Management Principle in the World —
    Michael LeBoeuf
If it ain't broke . . . BREAK IT! — Robert J. Kriegel
The Joy of Working — Denis Waitley
Leaders — Warren Bennis & Burt Nanus
Leadership is an Art — Max DePree
Mastery — George Leonard
Maximum Achievement — Brian Tracy
On Becoming a Leader — Warren Bennis
Positive Addiction — William Glasser
The Road Less Traveled — Dr. M. Scott Peck
The Strength to Strive — David Pease
The Tao of Pooh — Benjamin Hoff
Transformation Thinking — Joyce Wycoff
A Whack on the Side of the Head — Roger Von
    Oech
Wishcraft — Barbara Sher
Zapp! — William Byham

The highest reward for a person's toil is not what they get for it, but what they become by it.

—Ruskin

GRADES

W hat the heck are all of these letters of the alphabet and symbols?

$$A+ \qquad C- \qquad D+$$

$$B- \qquad A-$$

$$C \qquad B+ \qquad A$$

Grades?

No.

These are letters of the alphabet randomly placed on this paper. Some of them have plus or minus after them. These are not grades because no one has earned them. Looking at the "A–" you don't feel a sense of satisfaction for any work you've done. You don't feel any pride in this collection of letters and symbols.

Grades are not just letters and symbols. Letters and symbols become grades when they are your return on your investment of time and energy.

Grades are not just what you see.
Grades are what you earn.
Grades are what you feel.

Not to have edges that catch
But to remain untangled,
Unblinded,
Unconfused,
Is to find balance,
And he who holds balance beyond
sway of love or hate,
Beyond reach of profit or loss,
Beyond care of praise or blame,
Has attained the highest post
in the world.

—Lao Tzu

WHY "TGIF"?

"TGIF", "HUMP DAY", and "BLUE MON-DAY." What awful phrases! We hear them all the time. Why?

We think (or have been programmed to think) the week begins with Monday. The week really begins with Sunday. We spend most of our time planning for the weekend—Saturday and Sunday, but the weekend is really Saturday.

Historically the week was considered to begin with a spiritual day of reflection and peace. Work would then begin on Monday. But people considered the start of the week on quiet Sunday. Sunday, the quiet day, was a mental preparation day.

Why do we focus on the work week and the weekend as two separate items? Doesn't it make more sense to consider the week beginning with a peaceful day to clear our minds and prepare for productive work and ending with Saturday—a vacation day for fun and celebration and positive indulgence?

I like that idea!

First keep the peace within yourself,
then you can also bring peace
to others.

— Kempis

"THE CHURCH"

I went to "the church" today. Admittedly, it was a long time since I had last been there. It felt really good. I travel a lot for my job, so it's hard to get to "the church." (I mean the actual building as "the church.") It felt great to get up early, get dressed and go to "the church." The simple fact that this morning all of the people in "the church" had devoted their time to specifically remind themselves of something greater than themselves is really a special event in itself.

I don't believe you have to go to "the church" to be spiritual. In fact, I believe the whole world is one big church. I don't know what you believe, but it is important to remind ourselves that there is always something greater than ourselves.

We get too consumed in ourselves and our own lives which seem so enormous. Making the special effort to go to "the church" is a healthy exercise.

Maybe you don't go to "the church" or share the same beliefs of people who are at "the church." That is fine. But the simple act of making ourselves go somewhere out of the ordinary for pondering thoughts above or greater than ourselves is important. Maybe it isn't "the church," maybe it is a park (which seems to me to be a much more appropriate place to ponder the world). Wherever you decide to visit, sit, watch, or think, make a special visit to that place. You will feel a renewed sense of self.

Hope you are overwhelmed and awed by the enormity of the world.

Happy pondering!!!

*To make headway, improve
your head.*

—B.C. Forbes

*Others will tell you to try to prove
you are right. I tell you to try to
prove you are wrong.*

—Louis Pasteur

*I have found power in the mysteries
of thought.*

—Euripides

THE JOURNAL OF WHY'S

Occasionally we hear, see, or feel something that "strikes us" as strange, funny, unjust, bizarre, etc. It might happen when we are in the middle of a complicated task or sitting on the couch. We all have these moments, or what I like to call BRAIN BUSTERS. In fact, this book is full of thoughts of my personal *brain busters.*

A *brain buster* occurs whenever you see something in a new way or when you stop and question "why." It can hit you like a ton of bricks or suddenly creep into your mind. *Brain busters* usually are accompanied or recognized by a feeling or some intuition. *Brain busters* occur when the world is giving you information that doesn't match what your brain thinks is true. The computer in your head— your brain—is telling you that it is receiving bad input.

This feeling may be irritating or even a nuisance, but *brain busters* are in fact moments to be celebrated. *Brain busters* occur because we are naturally curious creatures. We try to make sense of situations and ultimately our world.

Even though we have these moments—these opportunities for enormous discovery—sometimes they disappear as fast as they occur. Why not explore these curious situations, statements, events or injustices? Why not discover why you think and feel the way you do? Why not create a "Journal of Whys?"

A Journal of Whys is your very own personal collection of questions you have about the world. You may have had a *brain buster* in 1996 and not find out how you truly feel about it until the year 2010. A Journal of Whys is a very special place to record the things you question. Your Journal of Whys can be whatever you want it to be. I suggest the Journal of Whys to you to use as a record. Maybe one day in June you have a strange encounter with a person and wonder why the situation occurred in the first place. Don't forget the situation and what happened. This can be a learning and growing experience. Write down your questions. Write down what doesn't make sense to you. No, you don't have to know the answers, but at least you have a question. At least you are examining— wondering how you feel about this huge world.

The next few pages are yours to experiment with a Journal of Whys. You may decide that this is a crazy idea and you want nothing to do with this type of journal. Great! But first let me ask you to try writing a few of your own questions you want to ask the world on the following pages. This can be the start of your Journal of Whys. The "whys" are not necessarily positive or negative. "Whys" just represent something that doesn't make sense or may be confusing to you. I have shared some of my own "whys" on the first few lines as an example. Play with it and use it however you feel best.

** THE JOURNAL OF WHYS **

$\mathbf{W}$hy don't I ask homeless people to live with me since I have a home?

Why do some people make other people feel guilty for things they can't control?

Why are dogs so loyal?

Why does America have so many names?

Why do both the mothers and fathers of so many families have jobs now?

Why do some people ignore me when I walk by them on the street?

Why do I think some people are more important to me than other people?

Why do some people belong to so many organizations but don't do anything to contribute to the organizations?

_____

_____

_____

_____

_____

_____

_____

What we have to do is to be forever curiously testing new opinions and courting new impressions.

—Pater

DO YOU WRITE? OR ARE YOU AFRAID OF THE RULES?

When was the last time you wrote something that you didn't have to turn in or wasn't an assignment? Yesterday . . . last week . . . last month . . . last year . . . never? Do you like to write? Or have you ever tried?

Writing was something I discovered after graduating from high school—when I didn't **have to** write. In fact, now I look forward to writing because now I don't have to worry about the rules. There are no standards or limits. I create what I want with pen and paper. It really is a fun adventure. Writing helps me think. In fact, I have some of my best conversations or discussions when my mind is racing and my pen is recording. But why don't people write?

Here is my theory . . . In school, particularly grade school, I learned mountains of knowledge, but I don't think I ever learned to write . . . I mean to write for myself. We read, "See Dick. See Jane. See Spot." We learned the words and what they meant. We learned to print and then cursive. Remember the special paper with two heavy lines, one on the top and one on the bottom separated by a dotted line to serve as a guide. That was fun paper! But not all of our writing lessons were fun. I remember being told that I was wrong because I put a little circle over my small "i" instead of just a dot. What a ridiculous rule! My "i" with the circle on top looked much prettier than the "i" with a little spot on top. But my teacher didn't think that mattered. That was one of the first writing rules I was forced to obey.

Then we learned grammar. More rules. "We was" is wrong. "I was" and "We were" are right.

The punctuation was simple when we just put a period at the end of a thought, but how confusing with ".,;— . . .:—?!" Ugh! The real clincher was the comma when we listed a group of things. The little grammar book told me it was optional (that means I decide) to put the last comma in before the word "and" or "or," but the teacher said I had to put it in or I would be wrong. Who was right? The grammar book or my teacher. And how could I find out? Confusion and conflict in my grade-school life!

Even when we had little paragraphs to write about ourselves or something we had done, the rules always seemed most important. My ideas were second to how I dotted my "i" or if I put in a comma in a series of items. No one said, "Wow, what a clever idea!" or "Gee, that sounds interesting!" Instead, the paper had marks (usually big, ugly, red ones) that pointed out my mistakes—where I broke the rules. I learned to dislike what I thought was writing. Now I understand that I never learned how to write. Sure we were assigned essays as students, but the rules of writing were most important. No one ever said, "Think about something wonderful and write. Just enjoy writing." We were always writing to simply use the rules. The rules were given more value than the interactive process of thinking and writing.

Now writing has a whole new personality for me. It is

a necessary activity for me. Writing has become an active way for me to think. My brain can hear or digest a small piece of information and wonder for hours how this information fits with my view of the world, or if it does not fit with my view of the world. Should I accept this information as truth or reject the information?

This book is a collection of mental conversations which have been written. Some of the ideas you might think are half-baked, which is wonderful. [If someone disagrees with me, at least I know they have listened to the information and choose to reject it. If people simply agree or nod their heads, sometimes I wonder if they really are listening or just agreeing to make me feel good.] All of these ideas are in my mind. Writing these ideas, conflicts and experiences literally helps me see what I am thinking. I have found no other more effective way to work through a question or challenge. But I had to discover this for myself. When I was supposed to be learning to write no one ever showed me why writing is important.

If you think you don't like to write maybe you aren't writing. Maybe you are just obeying those rules. When you write for your own benefit no one else sees what you write. No one sees where you put your commas and periods or even if you have **any** commas or periods. Writing doesn't equal grammar or penmanship. Writing is an active way to record your interpretation of an experience or to share your perceptions of the world. Forget the rules when you are writing for yourself. The rules don't give value to your ideas.

The ideas of this book were written with no rules. In fact, most of this was written over a long period of time when I didn't think anyone would see these ideas. The ideas were written and much later edited for printing. The ideas are the same as they were when they were first written, now they just look a little better.

Try writing about something you have wondered—a question, a challenge, an injustice. Forget the rules and enjoy yourself!

WRITE ON!

INSPIRING
THOUGHTS

INSPIRING THOUGHTS

The future belongs to those who believe in the beauty of their dreams. —*Eleanor Roosevelt*

You can't build a reputation on what you're GOING to do. —*Henry Ford*

Progress always involves risk; you can't steal second base and keep your foot on first. —*Wilcox*

The heights by great men reached and kept were not attained by sudden flight, but they, while their companions slept, were toiling upward in the night. —*Henry Wadsworth Longfellow*

Men for the sake of getting a living forget to live. —*Margaret Fuller*

We act as though comfort and luxury were the chief requirements of life, when all that we need to make us happy is something to be enthusiastic about. —*Charles Kingsley*

Everybody is ignorant, only on different subjects. —*Will Rogers*

Do not wish to be anything but what you are, and try to be that perfectly. —*De les*

Dream what you dare to dream. Go where you want to go. Be what you want to be.

To laugh often and much; to win the respect of intelligent people and the affection of children; to earn the appreciation of honest critics and endure the betrayal of false friends; to appreciate beauty; to find the best in others; to leave the world a bit better, whether by a healthy child, a garden patch or a redeemed social condition; to know even one life has breathed easier because you have lived. This is to have succeeded. —*Ralph Waldo Emerson*

Act as though it were impossible to fail.

Treat a man as he is and he will remain as he is. Treat a man as he can and should be and he will become as he can and should be. —*Goethe*

Today's preparation determines tomorrow's achievement.

The most incomprehensible thing about the world is that it is comprehensible. —*Albert Einstein*

Creative activity could be described as a type of learning process where teacher and pupil are located in the same individual. —*Arthur Koestler*

Once a word goes out of your mouth, you can never swallow it again. —*Russian proverb*

Far better it is to dare mighty things, to win glorious triumphs even though checkered by failure, than to rank with those poor spirits who neither enjoy nor suffer much because they live in the gray twilight that knows neither victory nor defeat. — *Theodore Roosevelt*

I think and think for months and years. Ninety-nine times, the conclusion is false. The hundredth time I am right. — *Albert Einstein*

Few people think more than two or three times a year. I've made an international reputation for myself by thinking once or twice a week. — *George Bernard Shaw*

In the last analysis, our only freedom is the freedom to discipline ourselves. — *Bernard Baruch*

Our quality of life depends on the quality of our leaders. — *Warren Bennis*

Let us admit the case of the conservative: if we once start thinking, no one can guarantee where we shall come out; except that many ends, objects and institutions are doomed. Every thinker puts some portion of an apparently stable world in peril, and no one can wholly predict what will emerge in its place. — *John Dewey*

Don't try to take on a new personality; it doesn't work. — *Richard Nixon*

The world is a tragedy to those who feel, and a comedy to those who think. — *William Shakespeare*

If you are distressed by anything external, the pain is not due to the thing itself, but to your estimate of it; and this you have the power to revoke at any moment. —*Marcus Aurelius*

Don't go around saying the world owes you a living; the world owes you nothing; it was here first. —*Mark Twain*

The great masses of the people will more easily fall victims to a great lie than to a small lie. —*Adolf Hitler*

Many persons have a wrong idea of what constitutes true happiness. It is not attained through self-gratification but through fidelity to a worthy purpose. —*Helen Keller*

Some people are discovered; others are found out.

We are discreet sheep; we wait to see how the drove is going, and then we go with the drove. We have two opinions: one private, which we are afraid to express; and another one—the one we use—which we force ourselves to wear to please Mrs. Grundy, until habit makes us comfortable in it, and the custom of defending it presently makes us love it, adore it, and forget how pitifully we came by it. —*Mark Twain*

If you can dream it, you can do it. —*Walt Disney*

A man is rich in proportion to the number of things which he can afford to let alone. —*Henry David Thoreau*

The first responsibility of a leader is to define reality. The last is to say thank you. In between the two, the leader must become a servant and debtor. That sums up the progress of an artful leader. —*Max DePree*

The obscure we see eventually. The completely apparent takes longer. —*E.R. Murrow*

Wisdom is merely knowing what to do next.

I who am blind can give one hint to those who see—one admonition to those who would make full use of the gift of sight: Use your eyes as if tomorrow you would be stricken blind. And the same method can be applied to the other senses. Hear the music of voices, the song of a bird, the mighty strains of an orchestra, as if you would be stricken deaf tomorrow. Touch each object you want to touch as if tomorrow your tactile sense would fail. Smell the perfume of flowers, taste with relish each morsel, as if tomorrow you could never smell and taste again. —*Helen Keller*

Learning is meant to be — active, passionate, and personal. —*Warren Bennis*

Do not be too timid and squeamish about your actions. All life is an experiment. —*Ralph Waldo Emerson*

I kept six honest serving men,
they taught me all I knew;
their names were What and Why and When
and How and Where and Who. —*Rudyard Kipling*

196

Here is the test to find whether your mission on earth is finished: If you're alive, it isn't. — *Richard Bach*

Imagination is more important than knowledge. — *Albert Einstein*

Where all men think alike, no one thinks very much. — *Walter Lippman*

There is no security on this earth, there is only opportunity. — *General Douglas Macarthur*

Life is no brief candle to me. It's a sort of splendid torch which I've got to hold up for the moment and I want to make it burn as brightly as possible before handing it on to future generations. — *George Bernard Shaw*

It is not who is right, but what is right that is important. — *Thomas Huxley*

If you have built castles in the air, your work need not be lost; that is where they should be. Now put the foundations under them. — *Henry David Thoreau*

In order to plan your future wisely, it is necessary that you understand and appreciate your past. — *Jo Coudert*

There are seeds of self-destruction in all of us that will bear only unhappiness if allowed to grow. — *Dorothea Brande*

How is it that many individuals, who possess only limited capabilities, manage to attract great admiration for extraordinary results? — *Kenneth Hildebrand*

Many of us spend our lives searching for success when it is usually so close that we can reach out and touch it. — *Russell Conwell*

One can never consent to creep when one feels an impulse to soar. —*Helen Keller*

You gain strength, courage and confidence by every experience in which you really stop to look fear in the face. You are able to say to yourself, "I lived through this horror. I can take the next thing that comes along." You must do the thing you think you cannot do. —*Eleanor Roosevelt*

Without goals, and plans to reach them, you are like a ship that has set sail with no destination. —*Dr. Fitzhugh Dodson*

Our greatest glory is not in never falling, but in rising every time we fall. —*Confucius*

Take a chance! All of life is a chance. The man who goes furthest is generally the one who is willing to do and dare. The "sure thing" boat never gets far from shore. —*Dale Carnegie*

Let your intentions create your methods and not the other way around. —*Benjamin Franklin*

Strong lives are motivated by dynamic purposes. — *Kenneth Hildebrand*

You don't have to like and admire your boss, nor do you have to hate him. You do have to manage him, however, so that he becomes your resource for achievement, accomplishment, and . . . personal success as well. *—Peter Drucker*

Unless you try to do something beyond what you have already mastered, you will never grow. *—Ronald E. Osborn*

The ancestor of every action is a thought. *—Ralph Waldo Emerson*

To be what we are, and to become what we are capable of becoming, is the only end of life. *—Robert Louis Stevenson*

Cherish your visions and your dreams as they are the children of your soul; the blue prints of your ultimate achievements. *—Napoleon Hill*

Ideals are like stars, you will not succeed in touching them with your hands, but like the seafaring person on the desert of water, you choose them as your guides, and, following them, you reach your destiny. *—Carl Shurz*

Remember that a person's name is to that person the sweetest and most important sound in any language. *—Dale Carnegie*

Our doubts are traitors, and make us lose the good we oft might win by fearing to attempt. *—William Shakespeare*

Quality is never an accident; it is always the result of high intention, sincere effort, intelligent direction and skillful execution; it represents the wise choice of many alternatives. —*Willa A. Foster*

Yesterday is a canceled check; tomorrow is a promissory note; today is the only cash you have — *so spend it wisely.* —*Kay Lyons*

We must be the change we wish to see in the world. — *Gandhi*

History has demonstrated that the most notable winners usually encountered heartbreaking obstacles before they triumphed. They won because they refused to become discouraged by their defeats. —*B.C. Forbes*

Success . . . seems to be connected with action. Successful people keep moving. They make mistakes, but they don't quit. —*Conrad Hilton*

Some people see things as they are and say "Why?" I dream things that never were, and say "Why not?" —*George Bernard Shaw*

Strive always to be like a good watch—open face, busy hands, pure gold, well—regulated, full of good works.

The most valuable of all talents is never using two words when one will do. —*Thomas Jefferson*

A diamond is a chunk of coal that made good under pressure.

Management is doing things right; leadership is doing the right things. — *Warren Bennis & Peter Drucker*

My philosophy is that not only are you responsible for your life, but doing the best at this moment puts you in the best place for the next moment. — *Oprah Winfrey*

The most important ingredient we put into any relationship is not what we say or what we do, but what we are. — *Stephen Covey*

Service is the rent we pay for the privilege of living on this earth. — *N. Eldon Tanner*

That which we persist in doing becomes easier — not that the nature of the task has changed, but our ability to do has increased. — *Ralph Waldo Emerson*

We must not cease from exploration. And the end of all our exploring will be to arrive where we began and to know the place for the first time. — *T.S. Eliot*

If there's anything I really believe in, it's the joy of learning and learning every day. — *Hesselbein*

For one human being to love another: that is perhaps the most difficult of all our tasks, the ultimate, the last test and proof, the work for which all other work is but preparation. — *Rainer Maria Rilke*

The world breaks all of us, and we grow stronger in the broken places. — *Ernest Hemingway*

The uniqueness of man—the superiority of man in the world of animals—lies not in his ability to perceive ideas, but to perceive that he perceives, and to transfer his perceptions to other men's minds through words. —*Albert Einstein*

Do not fear death so much, but rather the inadequate life. —*Bertolt Brecht*

Always bear in mind that your own resolution to success is more important than any other one thing. —*Abraham Lincoln*

To lead, One must follow. —*Lao Tzu*

PATTY HENDRICKSON, Certified Speaking Professional, works with organizations that want to grow leaders and with people who want more out of life. As a keynote speaker and leadership facilitator since 1987, Patty has shared enthusiastic messages throughout the world to more than 100,000 people.

Patty's programs on leadership, teams and self-esteem for professionals and students of all ages are known for their enthusiastic approach, combining practical information with fun.

If you're looking for an energizing keynote speaker or workshop leader, ask for Patty's free promotional information. *Her energy inspires, so her message sticks!*

Patty Hendrickson
Hendrickson Leadership Group, Inc.
N601 Lost Ridge Rd.
Lacrosse, WI 54601
800-557-2889
Patty@pattyhendrickson.com
www.pattyhendrickson.com